The **GI**
DIET PLAN

The GI

DIET PLAN

Use the glycaemic index to lose weight

and gain energy

Helen Foster

ℬℬ **Bounty**
Books

First published in Great Britain in 2004 by
Hamlyn, a division of
Octopus Publishing Group Ltd

This edition published 2005 by Bounty Books,
a division of Octopus Publishing Group Ltd
2–4 Heron Quays, London E14 4JP

Reprinted 2005 , 2006

Copyright © Octopus Publishing Group Ltd 2004

ISBN-10: 0-753711-92-3   ISBN-13: 978-0-753711-92-7

A CIP catalogue record for this book is available from the British Library

Printed and bound in China

The Gi Diet Plan is meant to be used as a general reference and recipe book to aid weight loss. However, you are urged to consult a health-care professional to check whether it is a suitable weight loss plan for you, before embarking on it.

While all reasonable care has been taken during the preparation of this edition, neither the publishers, editors, nor the author can accept responsibility for any consequences arising from the use of this information.

NOTES

Both metric and imperial measurements are given for the recipes. Use one set of measures only, not a mixture of both.

This book includes dishes made with nuts and nut derivatives. It is advisable for those with known allergic reactions to nuts and nut derivatives and those who may be potentially vulnerable to these allergies, such as pregnant and nursing mothers, invalids, the elderly, babies and children, to avoid dishes made with nuts and nut oils. It is also prudent to check the labels of pre-prepared ingredients for the possible inclusion of nut derivatives.

Meat and poultry should be cooked thoroughly. To test if poultry is cooked, pierce the flesh through the thickest part with a skewer or fork – the juices should run clear, never pink or red.

All the recipes in this book have been analysed by a professional nutritionist. The analysis refers to each serving.

contents

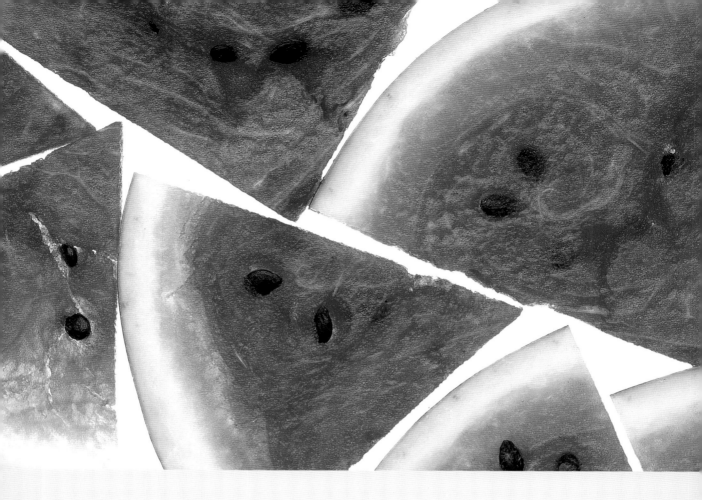

Introduction

What did you eat today? Does toast and juice for breakfast, a sandwich for lunch, and a bowl of pasta for dinner sound familiar? It probably does, as it is the staple diet of so many of us. Most people would think it was also a pretty healthy diet, as it is low in fat and high in energy-giving carbohydrates. It will therefore surprise you to discover that by eating such a diet you could be increasing your risk of heart problems, diabetes, weight gain and possibly even some cancers. The truth is that everything we have learned about nutrition over the years is currently being turned on its head.

Too much of a **good thing**

Back in our grandparents' day, the average person ate 10–13 different types of food a day; today the average person eats 6–8. And the majority of these foods come from one main food group – carbohydrates, and primarily white bread, potatoes, cakes, biscuits and sugary treats. While they may taste good and be easy to eat, these foods create reactions in our bodies that put the entire system out of balance. This is bad news as balance is what our entire system craves – scientists call it homeostasis. The result of imbalance is day-to-day problems such as fatigue, mood swings and sugar cravings – plus an increased risk of a number of different health problems in the future.

This may not sound new to you. After all, high-protein diets are now very popular, and in these diets carbohydrates are severely restricted or even banned entirely. And while it's true that these plans help us overcome the side effects of carbohydrate overload, they can bring with them problems of their own such as bad breath, digestive disorders and overworked kidneys. The results are no less confusing to our systems than what's gone before. There is, however, a better way to eat which stops all the confusion and allows your body to develop a sense of balance without any harmful side effects. It is based on what scientists call the glycaemic index, or GI.

A new way of eating

Put very simply, the glycaemic index measures how the food you eat reacts in your body. By following a low-GI diet, you choose foods that create only a positive reaction. It sounds simple – and it is. So simple, in fact, that nutritionists are hailing GI as the buzzword for eating in the 21st century, and researchers at the prestigious Harvard University in the USA are producing guidelines based around a low-GI diet which they hope will soon become the national blueprint for health. Forward-thinking countries like Australia are actually marking food packaging with a GI rating to help consumers make the right choice. Eating a low-GI diet is the ultimate way forward when it comes to boosting your health.

GI EXPLAINED

This chapter will clearly explain exactly what the glycaemic index is all about and why it has so many positive effects in your body.

You will discover all the health-boosting benefits that a low-GI diet can bring, everything from reducing your risk of heart disease to cutting your chance of developing wrinkles.

Finally, in this section you will be able to take a quick and easy test to show how your current diet compares, giving you a great baseline to work from when it comes to improving your diet, your body and your mind.

What is **GI**?

Every day your body has to take over 10,000 steps, think 40,000 thoughts, pump 36,000 litres (8,000 gallons) of blood round your system and deal with all the stresses and strains of modern life. To do this it needs energy – and it gets that energy from food.

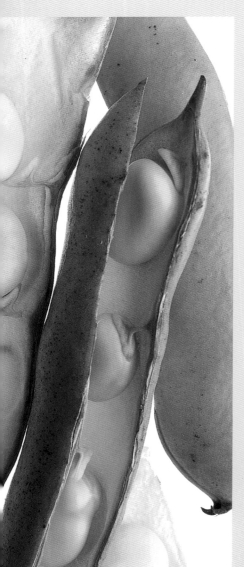

The secret of glucose and the **glycaemic index**

The body's preferred fuel is a sugar called glucose, which it makes from starches and sugars (carbohydrates) found in the food that we eat. Glucose is made in the liver after the food has been digested in the stomach. The converted glucose is then sent to the body's cells where it is either burned immediately as we run, walk or even think, or stored in the muscles and fat stores for later use. This happens with just about every food that contains carbohydrates, whether it is a plate of spinach or a plate of doughnuts. What differs is exactly how fast this reaction happens – and in very simple terms the glycaemic index is a measure of that speed. Foods with a high glycaemic index (known as high-GI foods) are converted rapidly to glucose, while foods with a low glycaemic index (low-GI foods) are converted more slowly.

'slowly does it'

Low-GI foods take longer to digest, so you feel full for longer

What has this got to do with our health?

The missing link is a hormone called insulin. When glucose is released into the bloodstream, it is the job of insulin to take it where it is needed. If the glucose is released slowly there is no problem – moderate levels of insulin are released and have time to 'think' about where that glucose is needed most and send it there.

However, if high levels of glucose enter the bloodstream, the body panics. It might need glucose for fuel, but too much can be harmful. It therefore releases high levels of insulin which quickly transfer the glucose to the fat stores where it can do no harm. This can lead to weight gain if it happens too often. But weight gain isn't the only consequence. If insulin levels are raised too often, the cells that normally respond to glucose become resistant to its signals. Less glucose is taken to where it is needed, and it remains in the bloodstream which causes cell damage, contributing to ageing, and other problems such as furring of the arteries. And because the cells aren't getting enough fuel (which in itself causes fatigue), the body triggers the release of more and more insulin to try to rectify things. This boosts resistance further, and after many years can even trigger Type II diabetes.

Turning things around

Switching to a low-GI diet reverses this process. By ensuring you eat only foods that cause a gentle rise in glucose in your bloodstream, you prevent the panic reaction and balance your system. For healthy people this reduces the risk of insulin resistance occurring, and for the estimated 25 per cent of people already suffering from the condition, it can give the cells enough of a break to allow them to resensitize. As you will see, the results can positively affect everything from your heart to your skin.

the glucose process

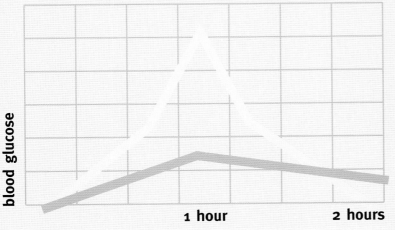

blood glucose

1 hour   2 hours

High-GI foods (such as white bread, baked potatoes, rice cakes and watermelon) are converted into glucose quickly

Low-GI foods (such as peanuts, sausages, wholemeal spaghetti and chocolate) are converted into glucose much more slowly

20 reasons
to eat low-GI foods

❶ Your heart will thank you. According to researchers at Harvard University, women who eat lots of refined carbohydrates have in their bloodstream 10 per cent less good cholesterol, which keeps the heart healthy, and 76 per cent more triglycerides, a particularly toxic form of fat, than those on low GI-diets.

❷ In a study at Yonsei University, in Seoul, South Korea, a group of men swapped white rice (high GI) for whole grains (low GI) and their levels of the amino acid homocysteine fell by 28 per cent in just six weeks. High levels of homocysteine are linked to heart problems and the development of Alzheimer's disease in later life.

❸ A high fibre content is a contributing factor in making a food low GI. This means that by increasing your intake of low-GI foods, you are more likely to be getting the 25–30 g (1 oz) of fibre health experts recommend daily. This will not only boost weight loss (fibre helps sweep fat calories out of the system), but may lower the risk of colon and other digestive cancers.

❹ By cutting sugary foods out of your diet, you will look younger. Many dermatologists believe that refined carbohydrates trigger inflammation in the skin. This creates high levels of free radicals (see page 35) which attack the collagen and elastin fibres that keep skin firm, causing poor skin tone and wrinkles.

❺ Reducing insulin levels can help acne and oily skin. According to research done at Colorado State University, high insulin levels lead to the release of higher levels of androgens (male hormones) in the system which trigger excess sebum production.

❻ According to the World Health Organization, the number of people suffering from diabetes will double by the year 2030. Switching our high-GI diets to low-GI plans could cut the number of potential sufferers dramatically.

❼ If you already suffer from diabetes, a low-GI diet can help you control your condition more effectively. Eight out of the nine studies which have looked at the effects in diabetics of switching to a low-GI diet, have found that it helps keep blood glucose levels more stable.

❽ A controversial theory by researchers at the University of Sydney has suggested that high-GI diets are linked to short sight. It is certainly true that the incidence of short sight is much lower in regions such as the Pacific islands where high-GI foods are far less common.

❾ Sugary foods attack your immune system. When fighting illness, the average white blood cell can destroy about 14 germs in an hour. However, when exposed to 100 g (3½ oz) of sugar that

number falls to 1.4 germs per hour, and stays like that for two hours. Low-GI eating will potentially cut the risks of ailments such as colds and flu.

❿ A diet rich in high-GI foods may increase the risk of breast cancer. The reason is that high insulin levels trigger an increase in insulin-like growth hormones which can encourage breast cancer cells to grow.

⓫ An increased incidence of pancreatic cancer has also been linked to a high-GI diet.

⓬ A low-GI diet can reduce the risk of stroke. Women who switched just one serving of refined carbohydrates to whole grains each day cut their risk of stroke by 40 per cent say researchers at Harvard.

⓭ Your energy levels rise dramatically when you go on a low-GI diet. The reason is that high-GI foods cause sudden peaks, then falls, in blood sugar which cause your energy levels to crash. The gentle rise that occurs with a low-GI diet creates a more steady energy flow.

⓮ You will have more stamina. Many exercisers think they need high sugar bursts to fuel their bodies, but in fact exercisers who stick to a low-GI diet throughout the majority of their training actually have better endurance.

⓯ Low-GI diets lead to happier people. A major mental benefit of carbohydrates is that they boost levels of the calming hormone serotonin. High-GI carbohydrates create a quick mood boost, but a mood crash follows soon afterwards, leaving you grumpy and jittery. Low-GI foods prevent this rollercoaster effect.

⓰ Steady energy levels are good for your brain. In an average day, 40 per cent of the glucose you make is used to power your brain. Slow, steady doses of glucose from low-GI foods, help to improve attention span and memory, according to research at the University of Wales.

⓱ Women can dramatically benefit from a low-GI diet as PMS (pre-menstrual syndrome) has been linked to erratic blood sugar levels. Also, high-GI diets are thought to be related to the condition Polycystic Ovary Syndrome (PCOS) that can cause fertility problems. Again, the ability of high insulin levels to increase levels of androgens (male hormones) in the body are believed to play a part here.

⓲ Your fertility may improve by eating a low-GI diet. Imbalances in blood sugar can reduce the body's ability to handle progesterone, the hormone that is vital for a successful pregnancy.

⓳ Children also benefit. Research at Massachusetts Institute of Technology found that children raised on diets high in refined sugars had lower IQs than those raised on low-GI diets. This is thought to be due to the reduced level of nutrients found in refined foods. High-GI eaters of any age have been shown to be lacking zinc, iron, folate and calcium.

⓴ You may even live longer. Studies show that people with high levels of vitamin C in their blood live up to 6 years longer than those with lower levels. A high-GI diet can decrease the amount of vitamin C you absorb from food by 25 per cent. This is because glucose and vitamin C enter cells in the same way and if there is too much glucose around, less vitamin C is absorbed.

What's your **GI factor?**

If you want to know whether you are at risk from health problems due to a high-GI diet, **answer the following questions and find out.**

How many servings of the following do you eat each day?
- White bread, bagels or rolls
- White rice or rice cakes
- Jacket or mashed potatoes, French fries or potato crisps
- Cakes
- Biscuits
- Cornflakes, rice cereals or honey-covered cereals

Score 1 point for every serving

When you eat vegetables, how likely are you to choose the following:
- Broad beans
- Parsnips
- Pumpkin
- Swede

Score 2 points for very likely, 1 point for occasionally, 0 points for never

Which of these is your most common breakfast?
a Cornflakes, rice cereals or similar
b Toast and jam
c Bacon and eggs
d Porridge and fruit
Score 2 points for a, 1 point for b, 0 points for c or d

How often are you hungry between meals?
a Only after breakfast
b After breakfast and lunch
c After all meals
d Never
Score 1 point for a, 2 points for b, 3 points for c, 0 points for d

If you gain weight, where does it tend to go on?
a Your stomach
b Your hips and thighs
c All over
Score 1 point for a, 0 points for b or c

How often do you get cravings for sugary snacks?
a Every day. I can set my watch by the 3pm chocolate run
b Only if I'm stressed, tired, or (for women) when I'm suffering PMS
c I never get cravings
Score 2 points for a, 1 point for b, 0 points for c

The **results**

More than 10 points

You are definitely on a high-GI diet and it looks as if you may already be suffering some of the symptoms. Being hungry within an hour or two of eating a meal is a classic sign of erratic blood sugar. Getting sugar cravings, particularly at 3pm when our energy levels naturally dip, is another common symptom. Finally, gaining weight around your middle is one of the most common symptoms that your fat stores are being controlled by insulin. You will dramatically benefit from switching to a low-GI plan.

5–9 points

While you are on a lower-GI diet than those scoring higher points, there are still places where you could improve your diet to harness all the health benefits a low-GI diet may bring. Whether it is by switching to lower-GI versions of your favourite carbohydrate foods, or combining those healthy choices that you do make with ingredients that lower their GI, you can maximize weight loss efforts and help balance mood, energy and cravings for sweet foods.

Less than 4 points

Well done; you are already likely to be eating a low-GI diet. However, you may not think you are harnessing all the benefits that this filling and healthy way of eating can bring. Perhaps you are not timing meals correctly, which is sapping your energy; or perhaps you are getting portion sizes wrong, reducing the effects of your healthy choices. Whatever the reason, you can turn things around by following the advice that follows.

All foods are **not** equal

The whole premise of the Easy GI Diet is that some foods create a faster rise in insulin production than others. Therefore, by choosing low-GI foods instead of high-GI foods you can balance insulin levels and prevent weight gain.

Obviously, to do this you need to know which foods are the best to choose. A few years ago this was thought to be easy – it was believed that so-called complex carbohydrates (such as bread, pasta and rice) were converted more slowly to glucose than simple carbohydrates (commonly thought of as the sweet sugars found in fruit, cakes and biscuits). However, the more we learn about the glycaemic index, the more we realize that this isn't quite true. In fact, there are six main elements that determine the GI of a food:

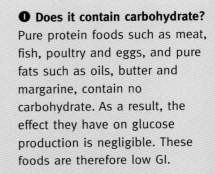

❶ **Does it contain carbohydrate?**
Pure protein foods such as meat, fish, poultry and eggs, and pure fats such as oils, butter and margarine, contain no carbohydrate. As a result, the effect they have on glucose production is negligible. These foods are therefore low GI.

❷ **How much starch does it contain, and in what form?**
The easiest ingredient for our body to convert into glucose is starch. When foods are raw, this starch is generally found in hard, compact particles that the body finds hard to break down. However, if something disturbs these starch particles (for example, milling into flour), the body finds it much easier to digest them and they turn into glucose faster.

❸ **How much fibre does it contain?**
Fibre slows the time it takes the body to break down a food. This is one reason why beans and pulses (which are wrapped in a fibrous shell) have such a low GI.

Some surprises

The combination of all the factors which affect a food's glycaemic index can throw up some surprising results. In the GI world...

- **Parsnips and pineapple can be fat-making foods**

- **Peanuts are better than potatoes**

- **Bacon is a diet food – bagels not so much**

- **Chocolate is equal to cherries**

- **Watermelon is as bad as waffles**

- **French bread should be eaten with as much care as French fries**

But this doesn't mean you are restricted to a diet of nuts, bacon and chocolate (as tasty as that might seem) – there is a whole host of GI-friendly foods for you to eat.

❹ What kind of sugar does it contain?

There are four main types of sugar, and they raise blood sugar levels at different rates. Foods with a high concentration of glucose (such as sports drinks) need no conversion, so they raise blood sugar rapidly. Fructose (the sugar in fruit), however, converts slowly; as does lactose which is the main sugar in dairy products. This gives the majority of foods containing either fructose or lactose a low GI. The fourth sugar, sucrose, has a medium GI.

❺ Does it contain fat?

As well as having no effect on glucose itself, fat slows the speed at which food leaves the stomach and reaches the liver, slowing glucose production. This is the reason why potato crisps have a lower GI than most other types of potato.

❻ How acidic it?

Foods can contain acid ingredients – citrus fruits like oranges or lemons are a good example of this. The tang they create on your tongue comes from the citric acid they contain. Other acidic ingredients include lactic acid in milk products, and added ingredients, such as vinegars, in pickled products. Just like fat, acidity slows a food's progress through the system, and therefore slows the rate at which it converts into glucose.

'make the right choices'

By choosing low-GI foods, you can balance insulin levels and prevent weight gain

GI facts about **carbohydrates**

When you are following a low-GI diet, the biggest changes that are likely to occur are in the following six foods: bread, breakfast cereals, grains, pasta, potatoes and rice. That is not just because they make up the majority of our diet, it is these foods that our body finds easiest to convert into glucose. But don't panic if you like your bread – unlike high-protein diets, the Easy GI Diet doesn't ban starchy carbohydrates. Instead, the idea is to switch your choices to those with the lowest impact on your blood sugar levels.

Bread

The average person eats around 2650 loaves of bread in their lifetime. Some days, it seems every meal we eat can contain some kind of bread product. This wouldn't be a problem if all of

those were low-GI breads, but the majority aren't. They are often white breads, including baguettes, ciabatta and panini, made from extremely finely milled flour particles that take no time at all to break down into glucose. Switching from white breads to other choices is therefore a key GI-lowering tactic – and the easiest way to choose your new bread is to think of the three F's:

Fibre
The more fibre a bread contains, the lower its GI. If you really want to eat white or brown bread, choose one with added fibre. A much better choice, however, is granary or wholegrain breads which contain whole wheat grains. These not only boost the fibre

content of the bread, but the hard husk around the wheat grains dramatically slows glucose conversion, making a low-GI food.

Finely ground – or not?
Most bread is produced by grinding the flour through steel grinders to produce very fine particles. Stoneground breads, however, are produced by crushing the wheat grains between two large stones to create larger, and less easily converted, particles – and therefore a lower GI.

Flour type
Choosing a bread made from an ingredient that has a lower GI than wheat leads to a more GI-friendly bread (see right).

The **good bread** guide

Here is a guide to how quickly different bread types can raise glucose levels. At the top of the list are those that convert slowest – and are therefore good choices. Lower down are the rapid converters that should be avoided.

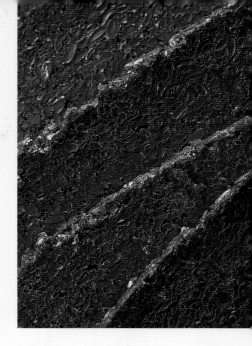

Low GI ↓ High GI

Barley bread (with whole grains)
Soya bread
Granary bread
Rye and pumpernickel bread (with whole grains)
Fruit bread
Wheat tortillas
White tortillas
Sourdough bread
Pitta bread (both white and brown)
Barley, rye or pumpernickel bread (without whole grains)
Stoneground white or brown bread
White or brown bread with added fibre
Brown or wholemeal bread or rolls
White bread or rolls
Bagels
Gluten-free bread
Baguette

The **good breakfast** guide

Best choices
Noodle-shaped bran cereals (turning bran into a flake raises its GI), traditional porridge oats (not instant)

Moderate choices
Muesli

Best avoided
Honey cereals, sugary cereals, flaked cereals (bran, corn or wheat), puffed cereals (wheat, corn or rice), wheat biscuits, instant porridge

Breakfast cereals

Breakfast is one of the most important meals of the day: studies show that regular breakfast eaters consume more nutrients and weigh less than those who skip breakfast. This is partly because eating breakfast prevents the hunger pangs which could make you reach for a less nutritious mid-morning snack. However, this will only work if you eat the right kind of breakfast.

A high-GI breakfast cereal is just as likely to leave you hungry as no breakfast at all. When researchers at Tufts University in the USA fed volunteers a high-GI breakfast, they ate almost twice as many snack calories later in the day as those fed a low-GI one. Many breakfast cereals are high-GI as the high levels of processing alter the starch bonds, making them easy to break down. Also, many breakfast cereals have high levels of added sugar or honey, which raise their GI value.

High-fibre cereals are the best option as they are usually low GI and have added health benefits.

Grains

It has been shown that when people start a low-GI diet, the variety of their diet increases by an average of nine new foods. The increased use of grains is one element of this, as many people experiment with grains rather than higher-GI staples such as rice and potatoes. It makes good health sense – most grains are high in essential B vitamins, and vital minerals like magnesium or phosphorus. Also, because they are subject to minimal processing, most grains have a low GI.

As grains are unfamiliar to many of us, here is a quick guide to what's what:

Barley (low GI)

Barley can be made into flour to create a very low-GI bread, and into flakes for porridge. However, the best choice for a low-GI diet is the smooth ivory grains of pearl barley. Pearl barley is rather like a cross between white and brown rice in both flavour and texture.

Buckwheat (low GI)

This grain has a very nutty flavour and a strong taste which means it goes well with meat or richly flavoured vegetable dishes. You will sometimes see it called kasha, which is a roasted form of the whole grain.

Bulgar wheat (low GI)

If you have ever eaten the Middle Eastern salad tabbouleh, you have eaten bulgar wheat as it is the primary ingredient. Unlike other grains, bulgar wheat doesn't need cooking, just steeping in boiling water for about 30 minutes, or according to packet instructions.

Couscous (medium GI)

This is made from semolina flour that has water added and is then rolled into tiny balls. It is normally found in quick-cook varieties which need only minimal cooking or just soaking. This additional processing increases the GI count, but in small portions it is still a valid, healthy food. It has a very mild flavour and should be accompanied by richly spiced or strongly flavoured foods.

Millet (high GI)

The very small grains and relatively low protein count make millet a high-GI food. Use barley or bulgar wheat instead.

Quinoa (low GI)

Pronounced *keen-wa*, this nutty tasting grain from Peru is actually a fruit. It takes about 15 minutes to cook and the grains change from white to transparent when it is done.

How to use grains

Most grains are simple to cook – just pop them into boiling water. The time they take to cook varies: barley can take 45 minutes, buckwheat takes 10–15 minutes, while couscous can be ready in as little as 3–4 minutes. Once cooked, they can be used in the following dishes:

- **Use instead of potatoes or rice as a side dish alongside meat or vegetable dishes**

- **Add to stews, soups or casseroles instead of potatoes or pasta to make a main meal**

- **Use as a great base for salads, helping to boost fibre count and keep you feeling full for longer**

- **Use in flour form to make bread (look out for barley, buckwheat and bulgar flours)**

- **Use in flake form as a breakfast cereal**

Pasta

Pasta is probably the food that confuses people most in the GI plan. On the face of it, it should be a high-GI food – it is packed with energy-giving carbohydrates, and in most cases it is a refined white food. However, virtually all pastas are low-GI foods because the flour used to make pasta (durum wheat) actually contains protein which slows its digestion. Also, the starch particles in pasta are left fairly intact, which also slows things down.

One point to bear in mind with pasta, however, is that many of us eat much larger portions than is recommended – and the greater amount of any food you eat, the more glucose it will produce. To estimate a portion more easily, a standard 75 g (3 oz) serving of spaghetti makes a bundle 2.5 cm (1 inch) across, while a similar serving of pasta shapes will fill half a cup. Also, the softer you cook your pasta the higher its GI index becomes – stick to eating all your pasta dishes al dente. This means the pasta is slightly firm as you bite it.

Gluten-free pasta

The exception to the low-GI rule is gluten-free pasta. Made of wheat-free flour, gluten-free pasta doesn't have the protein protection that durum wheat provides.

Noodles

Some Asian noodles – udon, for example – are made from a more glutinous form of wheat flour than other types and this raises their GI rating. Rice noodles follow rice in having a high GI. Soba noodles, which are made from part buckwheat, part wheat, are a lower-GI choice. If you do want to eat noodles, choose glass noodles, also known as bean thread noodles, cellophane noodles and harusame noodles. These are made of beans and have a very low GI.

Yams or sweet potatoes?

These root vegetables are known by different names in different countries. Yams and sweet potatoes are both low GI, so they are worth looking out for and including in your diet. Here's a brief guide to the differences between them:

• **Yams** are large vegetables with a thick, brown, knobbly skin, and a dry, white, purple or red flesh. They are usually found only in ethnic supermarkets.

• **Sweet potatoes** are smaller, orange- or yellow-fleshed vegetables, with a thin orange or brown skin, They are sometimes known as kumura.

Potatoes

Despite being a great source of vitamin C, potassium and the anti-ageing nutrient glutathione, potatoes do score poorly on the GI plan, with most varieties coming out as high-GI foods. The reason is believed to be their high starch content – borne out by the fact that new potatoes (which are the only potatoes to have a low GI) have lower levels of starch when they are picked than the same potatoes left on the plant to grow. Therefore, choose new potatoes for the majority of meals on the low-GI plan, or swap potatoes for some other form of low-GI carbohydrate.

The other option is to use sweet potatoes, which have a medium GI and can be roasted, mashed or chipped in just the same way as regular potatoes – but actually provide even more nutrients. In fact, when the US Center for Science in the Public Interest ranked vegetables in order of their content of fibre and six vital nutrients (vitamins A and C, folate, iron, copper and calcium) sweet potatoes came out top of the lot. Yams are also a good potato substitute and have a slightly lower GI, but they don't contain as many vitamins as sweet potatoes.

Rice

The GI content of rice depends primarily on which of two types of starch it contains – amylose, which is tightly bonded together, or amylopectin, which is more branched out. Because of its tight bonds, amylose tends not to break down as easily as amylopectin, so types of rice high in amylose have a lower GI than those high in amylopectin.

So how do you tell which your rice is? The theory is that if the grains stick together it is a high-GI rice; if they don't it is a lower one. However, the new easy-cook rices have made this test almost impossible for anyone but a rice expert to use. It is simpler to remember to choose those types of rice with a medium-GI content (see right).

Rice guide

High-GI rice
Any rice that takes less than 10 minutes to cook, jasmine rice, or sticky rice

Medium-GI rice
White rice, brown rice, wild rice, basmati rice

Low-GI rice
There is no such thing as a low-GI rice

'sticky or not?'

The theory is that if rice grains stick together, it is a high-GI rice, if they don't it is a low one

Carbohydrate snacks

We have become a snacking generation – in Europe alone, 1.4 million tonnes of snacks are eaten each year, while in the USA almost one-fifth of daily calories come from snack foods such as biscuits, cakes, chocolate and potato crisps. This is bad news as most snacks have a high GI – and the constant drip, drip, drip of sugar into the system is a major cause of increased insulin levels.

When it comes down to it, most sugary snacks (cakes, waffles, doughnuts, scones) have a high GI. Others, like biscuits or muffins, have a medium GI. But all contain high levels of harmful fats called transfats (see page 31). It would be sad to include these foods in a diet with as many heart-friendly health benefits as eating low GI.

Savoury snacks

A snack doesn't need to be sweet to raise glucose levels too quickly. Rice cakes, for example, a staple snack for the health conscious, have a very high GI because the rice is processed to make it into biscuit form and the starch particles become extremely easy to break down. Pretzels and popcorn suffer the same fate. Potato crisps have only a medium GI because their high fat content slows their conversion. However, they too suffer from the bad-fat problem (see page 31).

What you can eat

This doesn't mean snacking is banned completely when you are eating a low-GI diet. In fact, it is encouraged – eating a small meal or snack every two hours keeps blood sugar levels even more stable than eating three large meals a day. You just need to choose the right foods. Those that do fit the low-GI, healthy fat principle include nuts, seeds, fruit, yogurt – and chocolate.

Chocolate – a paradox

Chocolate has a low GI because of its high concentration of dairy products, its high fat content and the fact that it contains sucrose which is relatively slow to be converted into glucose. On top of this, chocolate is actually quite a healthy food as it contains high levels of antioxidants – as many as heart-healthy red wine. As a result, a little chocolate is allowed on the low-GI diet.

Remember, though, that added sugar-based ingredients like caramel or nougat will cause the GI to rise from low to medium. Stick to simple chocolate bars – particularly those made from dark chocolate.

Snack guide

High-GI snacks
Boiled sweets, doughnuts, jelly beans, chewy fruit sweets, popcorn, pretzels, rice cakes

Medium-GI snacks
Biscuits, corn chips, potato crisps, ice cream, chocolate bars with added caramel or nougat, muesli bars, muffins (plain or fruit)

Low-GI snacks
Nuts, seeds, chocolate (milk, white and plain), sponge cake, yogurt

Carbohydrates at a glance

High-GI carbohydrates
Breads Bagels, baguettes, gluten-free bread, white bread and rolls
Cereals Flaked cereals (corn, wheat or bran), honey-coated cereals, puffed cereals, instant porridge
Grains Millet
Pasta and noodles Gluten-free pasta, rice noodles
Potatoes Baked, French fries, mashed (real or instant)
Rice Fast-cook varieties, jasmine rice, sticky rice
Sweet snacks Boiled sweets, doughnuts, jelly beans, chewy fruit sweets, waffles
Savoury snacks Popcorn, pretzels, rice cakes

Medium-GI carbohydrates
Breads Barley, rye or pumpernickel bread (no grains), brown bread, fruit bread, pitta bread, sourdough bread, white tortilla wraps, white or brown bread with added fibre, stoneground bread
Cereals Bran cereal with fruit, muesli (low sugar and regular varieties), wheat cereal
Grains Couscous
Pasta and noodles All types of pasta, soba noodles, udon noodles
Potatoes Crisps, sweet potatoes
Rice Basmati, brown, risotto, white, wild
Sweet snacks Biscuits, chocolate bars containing caramel or nougat, ice cream
Savoury snacks Potato crisps, corn chips

Low-GI carbohydrates
Breads Granary bread and rolls, barley breads, rye or pumpernickel bread with grains, soya bread, wheat tortilla wraps
Cereals Bran strands, porridge
Grains Barley, bulgar wheat, buckwheat, quinoa
Pasta and noodles egg noodles or glass noodles (cellophane or bean thread noodles)
Potatoes New potatoes, yams
Rice There are no low-GI rices
Sweet snacks Milk, plain or white chocolate, yogurt, low-fat ice cream
Savoury snacks Nuts and seeds

GI facts about
fruit and vegetables

These vital health foods are a major part of any low-GI diet – and here's why.

Fruit

As a general rule, fruit is a low-GI food. This might surprise you as it usually tastes sweet, and it is digested very quickly. However, the fact that the main sugar in many fruits is fructose gives us a major metabolic advantage, as it has to be converted into glucose before it can be used. This prevents the sudden peak in blood sugar that can cause rapid insulin release.

What affects the GI of a fruit?

Acidity Generally, the more acidic a fruit is, the lower its glycaemic index. This is good news for fans of sour fruit like grapefruit, lemons and limes. However, many sweet fruits, such as kiwi fruit and oranges, also have high acidity.

Fibre content Fruits are high in soluble fibre, the type that has been shown to lower GI count. Generally, fruits with the highest soluble fibre content (apples and pears, for example, that are high in the fibre pectin) are those with the lowest GI. Pectin is also an appetite-suppressor.

Fructose content Fruits generally contain a mixture of three sugars: fructose, sucrose and glucose. The more fructose (and less glucose) a fruit contains, the lower its GI count. This is why watermelon, which is high in glucose, has a higher GI than other fruits.

Processing The processing involved with canning fruit alters its make-up, softening the fibrous strands within it. This makes the fruit easier to break down and slightly increases the rate at which glucose is created. Many fruits are canned in syrup which can contain fast-release sugars, and raise GI from low to medium.

Fruit juice also has a higher GI than the fruit it was extracted from as the fibre has been removed. Dried fruit generally raises blood sugar faster than the raw fruit it is made from.

Fruit guide

High-GI fruits
Watermelon, dates

Medium-GI fruits
Apricots (fresh and canned), bananas, cantaloupe melon, figs (fresh and dried), red grapes, mango, papaya, peaches (canned in syrup), pears (canned in syrup), raisins, sultanas

Low-GI fruits
Apples, dried apricots, avocado, blackberries, blueberries, cherries, grapefruit, white grapes, kiwi fruit, citrus fruits, peaches (fresh and canned in juice), pears (fresh and canned in juice), plums, prunes, raspberries, strawberries, tomatoes

Vegetables

Like fruit, the majority of vegetables are low-GI foods. This is because, despite the fact that many are classed as carbohydrate foods, the actual amount of carbohydrates they contain is very small – and in most cases, they are not types that cause rapid rises in blood sugar. On top of this, the fact that most vegetables are very high in fibre, a known GI-inhibitor, means that most vegetables can be seen as a free food on a low-GI diet.

There are, however, some exceptions to this – notably starchy root vegetables such as beetroot, parsnips and swede, or sweet vegetables like pumpkin, which are medium- or high-GI foods. In fact, parsnips have a higher GI than jelly beans. This doesn't mean that beetroot and parsnips are banned forever, though. One of the criticisms of the glycaemic index is the way that it is measured. To determine a food's GI, researchers measure a serving of the food that contains 50 g of carbohydrate. And it takes a very large quantity of parsnip or beetroot to give you 50 g of carbohydrate. If you eat less than this, and you will, the reaction will not be as severe. So, as long as portions are kept moderate, and you don't eat them for every meal, there is no reason to completely ban high-GI vegetables from your diet entirely.

Cooking and processing vegetables

In all cases, the glycaemic index is slightly raised when vegetables are cooked or processed – but the change is so minimal it won't make a huge difference to your blood sugar levels. After all, some vegetables are more nutritious when cooked, canned or frozen. For example, we get three times more betacarotene from cooked carrots than raw ones as heat softens the tough cell walls, making it easier for us to absorb the goodness within. Pumpkin, green beans and broccoli are also more nutritious when frozen or canned.

Vegetable guide

High-GI vegetables
Parsnips, pumpkin, swede, turnips

Medium-GI vegetables
Beetroot, corn-on-the-cob, sweetcorn kernels

Low-GI vegetables
Alfalfa, artichokes, asparagus, aubergine, bean sprouts, broccoli, Brussels sprouts, carrots, cabbage, cauliflower, celery, courgettes, cucumber, endive, fennel, garlic, green beans, kale, leeks, lettuce, mangetout, mushrooms, onions, okra, peas, peppers, rocket, radicchio, radish, spinach, Swiss chard, watercress

'low-carb, high-fibre'

Most vegetables can be seen as a free food on a low-GI diet

GI facts about
protein foods

The principal factor in determining the glycaemic index of a food is whether or not it contains carbohydrates. Pure protein foods, such as meat, fish and poultry, contain no carbohydrate and so have a low GI. However, there are some foods that contain high levels of protein, but also some level of carbohydrate, and therefore have a higher GI rating.

Beans and pulses

Most of us don't eat enough of these vital health foods – but we should. A diet that contains regular servings of legumes has been shown to lead to lower cholesterol levels, to help balance hormones in women, possibly reducing the risk of breast cancer. And, according to researchers at Australia's Monash University, legumes are the number one protector of longevity.

In terms of the GI diet, beans and pulses are also great foods, as most of them have a low GI due to the fibrous coating around them which slows conversion. Don't forget also that these foods don't just have a low GI in their natural form – tofu and other meat-replacement products made from soya, hummus or falafel made from chickpeas, and soups or dhal made from lentils all have a low GI as well.

Beans and pulses guide

High-GI pulses
Broad beans (fava beans)

Medium-GI pulses
There are no medium-GI pulses

Low-GI pulses
Baked beans, black beans, butter beans, chana dhal, chickpeas, edamane, haricot beans, kidney beans, lentils, soya beans, split peas

Dairy products

Again, while many of us believe these to be pure protein foods, the sugar lactose which many dairy products contain will be converted into glucose in the body. The good news is that these sugars are converted slowly, making dairy foods like milk, cheese, yogurt – and even low-fat ice cream – low-GI food choices. The only exception to this rule is condensed milk which commonly has other sugars added to it, but this is unlikely to be a staple part of your diet.

Nuts and seeds

The combination of protein and fats gives nuts and seeds their low GI – but this isn't the only reason these foods are recommended as part of the low-GI plan. They are also vital sources of the healthy fats our bodies need to stay healthy, look good – and even lose weight. To convince you of their health benefits even further, a study showed people eating 150 g (5 oz) of nuts each week were associated with living longer than those who didn't.

Some nutritionists describe seeds as a superfood, citing the fact that if a plant can grow from a seed, imagine what a powerhouse of nutrients and energy it must be. Nuts like peanuts, cashews, brazils or walnuts, and seeds like pumpkin or sunflower can easily be eaten by the handful as a snack or be sprinkled over salads. Also remember that spreads and dips made from nuts or seeds, such as peanut butter and tahini, will also have a low GI and can make great alternatives to butter or margarine. If you are watching your weight, though, remember nuts and seeds can be calorific.

Watch points

As with all processed products, the amount of sugar added to a food will vary – and increase its GI count. Soya milk, for example, commonly has sugar added. To ensure you are using a low-GI product, choose brands with less than 4 g of carbohydrate per 250 ml (8 fl oz) serving. This will be listed on the nutrition label, and most good brands will be labelled 'unsweetened'.

Another area that can alter GI is the addition of coatings, such as breadcrumbs or batter, to protein foods like chicken or fish, or the wheat used to bulk out burgers and sausages. Although amounts are usually so small that the difference is negligible, pure protein foods are healthier.

Pure proteins

All of the following foods can be seen as free foods on a low-GI diet (though watch fat counts carefully if you are dieting, or want to improve heart health).

- Anchovies
- Bacon
- Beef
- Chicken
- Clams
- Cod
- Crab
- Duck
- Eggs
- Gammon
- Goose
- Haddock
- Halibut
- Ham
- Kippers
- Lamb
- Liver
- Lobster
- Mackerel
- Monkfish
- Mussels
- Pilchards
- Plaice
- Pork
- Prawns
- Salmon
- Sardines
- Sea bass
- Skate
- Squid
- Sole
- Swordfish
- Trout
- Tuna
- Venison
- Veal

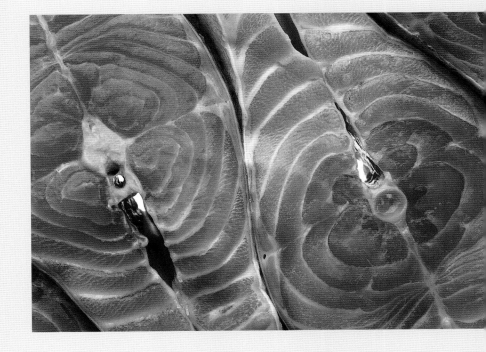

Drinks

It is not just solid food that turns to glucose in our systems – drinks do too. It is easy to consume them and forget about their potential effects on our health and weight. Choosing low-GI drinks is just as important as low-GI foods.

A note about **coffee**

Recent research from the Netherlands has revealed that the caffeine in coffee can actually increase the chance of cells becoming resistant to insulin – therefore increasing the amount your body is likely to secrete. As a result, caffeine is not a good choice for a low-GI diet.

The problem is that many of us can actually be addicted to caffeine – and when we come off we suffer headaches. However, if you wean off caffeine slowly you can quit it without symptoms. To do this, replace one-quarter of each cup of coffee you have each day with decaffeinated. Do this for three days, which is how long it takes your body to become accustomed to the new level. On the fourth day, replace another quarter of the cup with decaffeinated. Repeat until you are drinking no caffeine at all, which should take 12 days.

Drinks and **GI**

Low GI

- Water
- Tea and herbal tea
- Milk
- Tomato juice
- Apple juice
- Carrot juice
- Pineapple juice
- Grapefruit juice
- Orange juice
- Cranberry juice
- Red wine
- White wine
- Lemon squash
- Orange squash
- Cola
- Fizzy orange drink
- High-energy sports drinks
- Beer

High GI

Alcoholic drinks

Alcoholic spirits, such as gin, vodka and whisky, are also best avoided. While they have very little effect on insulin – and are therefore technically low GI – a high consumption of spirits is linked to other health problems.

Red wine is a better choice than spirits. Although it has a medium GI value, it contains antioxidants, which are good for your heart.

The **fat** factor

Many high-fat foods – chocolate, nuts, meat, dairy products, for example – are also low-GI. This is because fat does not raise blood sugar levels. In order to be healthy, a low-GI diet needs to include the right types of fat.

Why some **fat** is good for you

Fat is essential for a healthy body. For starters, without it you wouldn't be able to process the fat-soluble vitamins A, D, E and K which help keep your eyes, bones, skin and brain healthy and fully functioning. Your body uses fat for energy, and to create healthy cells and hormones, which regulate everything from how we feel pain to women's menstrual cycles. Without some fat your body won't look or feel good, but you need to make sure you are getting the right types.

Types of **fat**

Foods can contain four types of fat: saturated, monounsaturated, polyunsaturated and hydrogenated. (Also known as transfats, hydrogenated fats are made when vegetable oils are processed into a solid fat through heating.) When you eat a food that contains fat, you take in the first three of above fats, and occasionally the fourth. What varies is the percentage of different fats the food contains: meat for example is higher in saturated fat than it is in polyunsaturated fat; oily fish is the opposite. It is this ratio, plus the presence of transfats, that determines whether we think a food is 'healthy' or not. On a low-GI diet, you are aiming to choose not only low-GI foods for the majority of your meals – but when those foods also contain fats, to pick those high in healthy fats rather than unhealthy ones.

The foods to **choose**

Focusing on foods containing healthy fats and minimizing intakes of unhealthy ones is the key to good health. The GI plan makes this easy as many foods containing saturated fat are also high sugar so already banned. However, you should always remove any obvious fat from low-GI foods such as red meat, avoid frying and choose low-fat dairy where possible.

Healthy fats

Monounsaturated fats:
- Olives
- Nuts
- Seeds
- Avocados
- Oils from the above

Polyunsaturated fats:
- Trout
- Salmon
- Mackerel
- Herring

Unhealthy fats

Saturated fats:
- Butter
- Meat
- Full-fat dairy products

Transfats:
- Hard margarines
- Cakes containing hard margarines
- Biscuits containing hard margarines

When **low GI** meets **high**

While it won't do you any harm to eat only low-GI foods, after a while life could get a bit monotonous. This, therefore, brings us to the best news of all about the Easy GI Diet – no food is completely banned. But if you eat a high-GI food, you should follow a few rules to help reduce its effect on blood sugar.

The **rules**

❶ When you eat a high-GI food, watch your portion size. Scientists calculate the glycaemic index of a food by feeding a volunteer the amount of the food that contains 50 g of carbohydrate. For celery, this amount is about 50 sticks, for rice it is 150 g (5 oz) of cooked rice, while for sugar it is 4 table-spoons. The more you eat of a food, the greater amounts of glucose will be produced; if you eat less, you'll create less. Therefore, by controlling your high-GI portion sizes, you can lower the amount of sugar produced.

❷ Every time you eat a high-GI food, accompany it with at least two low-GI foods of the same, or a larger, quantity. This lowers the average GI of a meal and again decreases the amount of glucose produced. In an ideal world, one of those foods would be a protein food like meat, poultry, fish, eggs, legumes, nuts or dairy products. The other would be fruit or vegetables. Therefore, if you have 25 g (1 oz) high-GI cornflakes for breakfast, accompany this with 100 ml (3½ fl oz) of skimmed milk and a sliced peach.

❸ Don't eat more than one high-GI food or two medium-GI foods a day – and ideally have less than this. While these rules make eating high-GI foods less damaging to your system, to truly allow your body to get back into balance you should skip high-GI foods as often as possible.

❹ If the meal allows it, add something acidic. Just as acid integrated into a food slows its conversion to glucose, so does acid added to a high-GI food. This means eating half a grapefruit with a high-GI breakfast, accompanying a meal containing rice with a side salad topped with vinaigrette, or sprinkling French fries with vinegar. You could even try drinking a glass of hot water with a squeeze of lemon or lime juice in it. The acid factor can reduce the GI of some high-sugar foods by 30 per cent.

Low-GI portions for **high-GI foods**

Potatoes 100 g (3½ oz)
Rice 75 g (3 oz) cooked weight (roughly 25 g /1 oz dried)
Bread 1–2 slices

Breakfast cereals 25 g (1 oz)
Root vegetables 100 g (3½ oz)
Popcorn and pretzels 25 g (1 oz)

The **GI pyramid**

There is a huge range of foods that you can eat on a low-GI plan, but how much of each should you eat each day? The traditional food pyramid, which most of us see as healthy, focuses primarily on starchy carbohydrates like bread, pasta and rice, recommending up to 11 servings a day. Even if you stuck to the lowest-GI versions of these foods, there would still be a lot of glucose in your system. Here is a GI-friendly pyramid to help with your eating plan.

Tailor-made diets

If you are not going to follow one of our specific diet plans, use the pyramid as a guide to giving back your body the balance it craves. And don't forget to follow these vital guidelines:

• **Remember all carbohydrates are not equal.** If you do nothing else, at least switch high-GI carbohydrate foods like white rice, white bread, sugary cereals and potatoes for lower-GI choices.

• **Eat at least three meals a day.** Skipping meals leads to drops in blood sugar that trigger cravings for high-GI foods. It is a good idea to include two low-GI snacks each day as well.

• **If you do eat a high-GI food, follow the guidelines opposite** to reduce its effects on your body.

GI pyramid

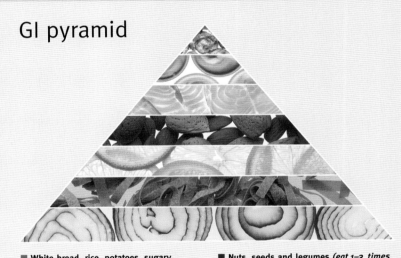

■ White bread, rice, potatoes, sugary treats like cakes and biscuits *(eat rarely)*
■ Dairy foods *(1–2 servings a day – ideally low-fat versions)*
■ Pure proteins such as meat, fish, poultry, eggs *(up to 2 servings a day – red meat no more than 1–2 times a week)*
■ Nuts, seeds and legumes *(eat 1–3 times a day)*, and oils made from these *(eat 1–2 times a day)*
■ Fruit *(2–3 times a day)*
■ Granary bread, grains, pasta and other low-GI starchy carbohydrate foods *(3–6 servings a day)*
■ Vegetables *(at least 5 servings a day)*

• **Remember fat is still bad for your body.** Choose foods low in saturated fat for most meals and include foods containing heart-healthy fats.

• **Drinks count.** Don't undo all your low-GI eating by washing it down with sugary sodas, fruit drinks or alcohol. If you do drink alcohol, stick to safe drinking limits.

GI ways to **boost health**

It has been shown in many studies that what we eat affects our health, with foods like fruit, vegetables, whole grains and legumes emerging as vital health protectors. By following any low-GI diet (which will be high in all of these), you can harness the protective power of food, lose weight and boost energy.

GI for **weight loss**

The point of the low-GI plan is to stop the rapid release of glucose into the system and decrease insulin production. This has a number of effects on weight. Firstly, insulin stops pushing excess sugar into your fat stores. Secondly, appetite falls, as insulin is actually an appetite stimulant. Thirdly, when insulin levels fall, the body releases another very important hormone called glucagon into the system.

Glucagon's job is to take glucose out of the fat stores and burn it up as fuel. The more often glucagon is released into your system, the more fat you burn. By eating low-GI foods, keeping insulin levels low, and cutting calories, you maximize the chances of glucagon being produced and thus putting your body into fat-burning mode. This immediately makes for more successful weight loss – but when you eat low GI you get other slimming benefits too.

Fill-up factor
You are less likely to be hungry on a low-GI diet than a high-GI one. When US researchers fed volunteers a low-GI meal, they ate 81 per cent less calories at their next meal than those fed a high-GI meal. This is partly because the appetite-increasing effects of insulin are suppressed, but also because low-GI foods tend to be higher in fibre and protein, both of which make you feel fuller for longer.

Craving control
Sugar cravings can derail even the most determined dieter – but they are far less likely to occur on a low-GI plan as you don't experience sudden rises and falls in blood sugar levels.

Vital vitamins
Some studies have suggested that people who eat a high-GI diet are deficient in zinc, iron, calcium and vitamin C. All of these are vital fat-burning nutrients. By going low GI, and increasing your intake of these vital fat fighters, you maximize weight loss.

Burning boost
Low-GI diets tend to be high in fibre, and for every gram of fibre you consume, your body burns 7 kcal (29 kj) to process it as it travels through your digestive system. By simply eating the recommended 25–30 g (1 oz) of fibre daily you can burn up to 200 kcal (840 kj).

GI for **anti-ageing**

There's no doubt that switching to a low-GI diet helps your health: reduced risk of diabetes, heart disease and some forms of cancer have all been linked to a lowered intake of high-GI foods. The reasons why are to do with sugar.

Soft, white – and deadly
Sugar is a naturally sticky substance – and particles of glucose in the blood are no exception to this. If sugar is left lingering in the bloodstream rather than being processed into fuel that can be burnt as energy, particles can actually stick to protein cells in the body, a process called cross-linking.

The collagen fibres that run through our bodies are especially prone to cross-linking. The fibres lose flexibility, become brittle and break down. In the skin, this leads to wrinkles. In the joints it leads to a lack of mobility. In the lungs it leads to decreased lung capacity and reduced oxygenation of the tissues, and in the blood vessels it leads to a stiffening, making the heart work that little

bit harder. These effects are the main signs of ageing.

But cross-linking isn't the only damage that sugar causes. Sugary foods also increase the number of free radicals in your system. When researchers at Buffalo University in the USA gave volunteers a meal containing 300 kcal (1260 kj) of sugar, the free radicals in their system increased by 140 per cent – that was more than when they ate a meal full of fat.

Time to fight back
Free radicals are atoms containing electrons that are missing a 'partner electron', and are the primary cause of ageing and illness in our bodies. They rampage around the body stealing electrons from other atoms. As this happens, healthy cells around the system get damaged, leading to ageing or changes in the cell that can trigger disease. By switching to a low-GI diet and eating less sugary foods, fewer free radicals are released into your system, which dramatically slows down the ageing process.

GI for **energy**

The rapid insulin rise that is triggered by high-GI foods means the glucose in our blood is rapidly pushed into the fat stores. Thus the glucose that should have gone to feed our muscles – and more importantly our brains – isn't used. This creates a lack of fuel in the system, resulting in low energy. If you then reach for more sugary carbohydrates, the problem is compounded further.

Carbohydrates also contain substances that the brain converts to a chemical called serotonin. This helps calm the body and creates a sense of wellbeing – in small doses. If large doses of serotonin are produced by eating a lot of high-GI carbohydrates, we begin to feel even sleepier.

By eating a low-GI diet, you change this immediately. Because the body is no longer subjected to sudden surges in sugar, it doesn't experience the sudden falls either. This alone keeps energy more constant. The fact that it reduces cravings for more carbohydrates also means your serotonin levels are kept under control, allowing you to harness the stress-relieving benefits of this chemical without experiencing the negative effects of overload.

the low-GI **plans**

There are four different low-GI plans, depending on what you want to achieve, whether it's weight loss, an energy boost, or a way to maximize your health.

The **Genius Weight-loss Plan** (see pages 38–67) and the **Vegetarian Weight-loss Plan** (see pages 68–89) show you how to lose weight the GI way. Simply follow the daily meal plans and the rules opposite.

The **GI Galvanizer Plan** (see pages 92–103) uses the principles of low-GI eating to maximize energy. Again, this is set out day to day, but it follows the rules on page 37 which are the key to eating low GI for energy.

The **GI for Life Plan** (see pages 104–117) is for those who generally feel good, but want to protect their health. It focuses on low-GI superfoods that are proven to boost immunity – helping to reduce the risk of major illnesses.

Using the **weight-loss plans**

Once you have the right mindset, losing weight is just a matter of burning more calories than you eat. The key to success is working out how many calories you need to eat in a day to create a safe calorie deficit. It is not a case of the more you cut a day, the better. If you cut too many calories your body actually slows down your metabolism, reducing the amount of calories you burn. So no matter how much weight you have to lose, you should cut only 500 kcal (2100 kj) from your recommended daily intake. You will lose 0.5 kg (1 lb) each week – which may sound slow, but means you won't be hungry, you can eat treats like chocolate, you are more likely to lose fat than muscle – and the weight is more likely to stay off.

The diet plans on the pages that follow provide 1500 kcal (6300 kj) a day. This is the amount that the average 70 kg (11 stone) woman in a sedentary job would need to lose weight. If you weigh more than this or are more active, you'll need to increase the amount of calories each day – if you weigh less, you'll need to decrease them. This is easy with the help of the GI charts (see pages 118–125).

Exercise

Exercise is particularly relevant when you're eating a low-GI diet as it decreases the insulin sensitivity of the cells, speeding up the rate at which your body starts producing glucagon. Each week you should aim to do at least 2 hours of exercise – at the gym, playing a sport or using the stairs in the office. You can plan your own activities, but the programme details an exercise task for each day.

Can I swap meals?

If you prefer to eat the suggestion for the evening meal at lunch – or vice versa – then do so. You can also swap or repeat days. Don't, however, swap meals from one day to another as each day has a set calorie count.

Calculating your **recommended intake**

First calculate your basal metabolic rate (BMR). To do this, multiply your weight in pounds by 10 (or should you be metrically minded, your weight in kilogrammes by 92.4). This is roughly how many calories (kcal) or kilojoules (kj) you burn a day at rest.

Of course most of us don't spend all day lying on the sofa so, depending on how active you are, you need to multiply that figure further.

- Sedentary job (office work) x 1.3
- Moderately active job (shop worker, homemaker) x 1.4
- Active job (postperson, traffic warden) x 1.5
- Very active job (builder, fitness trainer, courier) x 1.7

This gives the total amount of energy you burn on an average day. You should be eating 500 kcal (2100 kj) less than this to lose 0.5 kg (1 lb) of weight a week.

The **eating for energy** rules

Not only will you be focusing on low-GI foods, you will also be tailoring the timing of those foods to ensure they give the most benefits to your body. This means following these four rules:

❶ **Always eat a fibre-filled breakfast.** Any breakfast refills energy stores used up overnight, but a fibre-filled breakfast also helps boost the digestion, making it easier to absorb energy-giving nutrients from other foods. It will also prevent constipation, a major cause of fatigue.

❷ **Add protein to every meal.** This creates even slower-burning energy, and helps counteract the negative effects of too many carbohydrates. Protein is particularly important at lunch. Our energy levels naturally dip around 3pm. If you eat a high-carbohydrate meal for lunch, this natural dip combines with sugar dips and serotonin boosts to create fatigue.

❸ **Focus on carbohydrates in the evening.** By eating a more carbohydrate-heavy meal in the evening, you produce serotonin when you need it most – before bedtime. This helps ensure a more restful night's sleep and less fatigue the next day.

❹ **Eat small meals every four hours.** Digestion takes its toll, and eating meals that are too large can be tiring. Eating three small

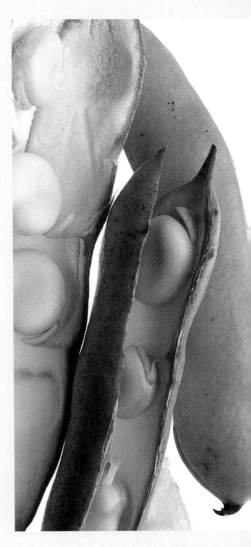

meals and two or three snacks each day prevents this.

You should eat at least three energy-giving foods a day, such as breakfast cereals, beans and pulses, oily fish, citrus fruit and berries, red meat and green leafy vegetables.

You will also see that, unlike the weight-loss plans, this diet doesn't have serving sizes. Eat enough so you feel full, but not overfull.

GENIUS WEIGHT-LOSS PLAN

This easy-to-follow plan does the hard work for you. Each day has a calculated calorie count, so all you have to do is follow the menus.

One of the major benefits of low-GI eating is that it is a great way to lose weight. No food is banned, so you don't get as many diet-destroying cravings. Most importantly, however, you actually rebalance the system of your body that controls fat storage and fat burning, ensuring the calories you cut really do end up as weight lost. Whether you want to lose a little or a lot, your slim new shape starts here.

day 1

This is your first day on the road to a slim new shape. The main thing you will notice is that you won't get hungry – in fact you may be eating more food than you normally do. Don't panic and don't skip meals – eating regularly fires up your metabolism and actually increases the amount of weight you lose.

breakfast

bowl of porridge
Use 75 g (3 oz) rolled oats and make according to packet instructions. Top with a large handful of blueberries, strawberries or sliced peaches instead of sugar

glass of unsweetened orange juice
150 ml (¼ pint)

snack

pot of low-fat fruit yogurt
150 g (5 oz)

handful of dried apricots
50 g (2 oz)

lunch

Moroccan Tomato and Chickpea Salad
(see recipe, right)

grilled chicken breast
150 g (5 oz)

ALTERNATIVE:
grilled chicken breast sandwich
150 g (5 oz) chicken breast served on barley, granary or soya bread, topped with sliced tomato and a little mustard

large salad
of celery, cucumber and grated carrot

snack

1 banana

10 brazil nuts

dinner

grilled tuna steak
150 g (5 oz) of tuna topped with 1 serving of Tomato and Pepper Salsa (see recipe, far right) or 2 tablespoons of prepared salsa. Serve with 100 g (3½ oz) of new potatoes and 75 g (3 oz) of mangetout

get a breath of **fresh air**

Take a 30-minute walk at your own pace. Aim for a level that gets you slightly out of breath, however, as this will burn more calories and strengthen your heart and lungs. To make it more fun, take a friend and walk round the local park catching up on the gossip.

Calories burnt: 150

moroccan tomato and chickpea salad

preparation time: 10 minutes, plus standing

serves 4

1 red onion, finely sliced

2 x 400 g (13 oz) cans chickpeas, drained and rinsed

4 tomatoes, chopped

4 tablespoons lemon juice

1 tablespoon olive oil

handful of herbs (such as mint and parsley), chopped

pinch of paprika

pinch of ground cumin

salt and pepper

1 Simply mix together all the ingredients in a large non-metallic bowl and set aside for 10 minutes to allow the flavours to infuse, then serve.

kcal: **200 (840 kj)**
protein: **12 g**
carbohydrate: **30 g**
fat: **5 g**
GI: **L**

nutrition tip:
Chickpeas are a great source of fibre and are also rich in magnesium and the B vitamin folate. Eating them regularly can lower your risk of heart disease and diabetes.

diet **power-up**

Chillies speed up the metabolism – and also help stop you being hungry. They are therefore a great addition to any diet programme.

tomato and pepper salsa

preparation time: 10 minutes, plus standing

serves 4

4 tomatoes, finely chopped

1 green chilli, finely chopped

1 red pepper, cored, deseeded and finely chopped

grated rind and juice of 1 lime

2 tablespoons chopped parsley

1 Mix together all the ingredients in a small bowl. Leave for 10 minutes to infuse, then serve.

kcal: **12 (50 kj)**
protein: **0.6 g**
fat: **negligible**
carbohydrate: **2.6 g**
GI: **L**

day 2

The key to a diet's success is sticking with it. Before you get started today look back at yesterday and think what went well and what didn't. Now look at why those things went wrong, and what would stop them happening again. Doing this kind of analysis allows you to develop slimming safety nets that mean you won't fall into the same trap twice.

breakfast

glass of unsweetened orange juice
150 ml (¼ pint)

2 slices of toast
Choose granary, barley or soya bread and spread with 2 teaspoons of ricotta cheese and 2 teaspoons of all-fruit conserve such as blackberry

snack

protein shake
made from 2 scoops of whey protein powder mixed with water, and 100 g (3½ oz) of tinned peaches in natural juice. Whey protein is a great low-fat, low-GI drink that can be found in health food stores and some supermarkets

ALTERNATIVE:
pot of low-fat fruit yogurt
150 g (5 oz)

lunch

small tub of low-fat hummus
about 125 g (4 oz), served with 3 rye crispbreads and crudités of carrot, cucumber, celery and cherry tomatoes

snack

handful of white grapes
50 g (2 oz)

dinner

Pork Balls with Tomato Sauce and Spaghetti
(see recipe, right)

ALTERNATIVE:
spaghetti bolognese
made using 75 g (3 oz) turkey or chicken mince per person, mixed with a 400 g (13 oz) jar of ready-made, fresh tomato pasta sauce. Serve with 75 g (3 oz), dry weight, of spaghetti per person

going up

Today's rule is never to take the lift or escalator. Climbing stairs gives your body a good workout – and even climbing down tones your legs. Each minute you climb burns 11 calories (about 7 coming down). Aim for 20–30 minutes of stair climbing today.

Calories burnt: 220–330

pork balls with tomato sauce and spaghetti

preparation time: 10 minutes

cooking time: 20 minutes

serves 4

375 g (12 oz) dried spaghetti

300 g (10 oz) minced pork

1 onion, finely chopped

1 garlic clove, crushed

½ teaspoon paprika

2 teaspoons tomato purée

700 g (1 lb 7 oz) jar passata

salt and pepper

1 Cook the spaghetti in lightly salted boiling water for 12 minutes, or according to packet instructions.

2 Meanwhile, mix together the mince, onion, garlic and paprika and season with salt and pepper. Shape the mixture into 12 balls.

3 Place the meatballs on a grill pan and cook under a preheated hot grill for 6–7 minutes, turning occasionally, until browned and cooked through.

did you know?

Eating a traditional high-carb diet is the equivalent of eating 2 cups of pure sugar a day. A low-GI diet produces dramatically less than this.

4 Drain the spaghetti, return it to the saucepan and stir in the tomato purée, passata and the meatballs. Season to taste with salt and pepper, heat through and serve.

kcal: **486 (2041 kj)**
protein: **27 g**
carbohydrate: **78 g**
fat: **9 g**
GI: **L**

nutrition tip:
Passata is a purée made from sieved tomatoes. It is a great source of lycopene, a vital antioxidant which has been shown to reduce the risk of lung, prostate and skin cancers.

day 3

By now you should be feeling some of the positive mental effects of the low-GI programme. One thing you should really notice is that pre- or post-meal mood swings have stopped, as you are not subjecting your body to sudden rises and falls in sugar levels that can make you grumpy and irritable.

breakfast

Pumpkin Seed and Apricot Muesli
(see recipe, right)

glass of unsweetened grapefruit juice
150 ml (¼ pint)

ALTERNATIVE:
muesli
50 g (2 oz) of any unsweetened muesli, topped with 150 ml (¼ pint) skimmed or soya milk

½ grapefruit

snack

½ mango
topped with 50 g (2 oz) low-fat cottage cheese

lunch

open tuna sandwich
made from 1 slice of granary, barley or soya bread, topped with 75 g (3 oz) of canned tuna in brine mixed with a little lemon juice and 1 teaspoon of low-fat mayonnaise, 1 sliced tomato and a handful of alfalfa sprouts

can or carton of lentil soup
400 g (13 oz)

snack

10 almonds

2 satsumas or kiwi fruit

dinner

grilled chicken breast
150 g (5 oz), served with 50 g (2 oz) of couscous (dry weight, cooked according to packet instructions) and 175 g (6 oz) of grilled vegetables – try a mix of aubergine, red pepper, courgette and onion

get **dancing**

Book a girls' night out and hit the local salsa, flamenco or disco class, or even a dance club. If you prefer to keep your moves to yourself, put on your favourite music and dance around the house for 20–30 minutes. Music's a great motivator for any exercise – studies show that a workout feels easier when it's done to music you enjoy.

Calories burnt: 100 for every 10 minutes

pumpkin seed and apricot muesli

motivation **booster**

Hunger on the low-GI plan is usually psychological (the foods have a high fill-up factor so real hunger is rare). The most common cause is that portion sizes for cereals, potatoes or other starchy foods may be smaller than you are used to which can make you think you should be hungry – so you are. If this is happening to you, switch to a smaller plate. It will look full, so you will feel full.

preparation time: 10 minutes

serves 2

50 g (2 oz) rolled jumbo oats

1 tablespoon sultanas or raisins

1 tablespoon pumpkin or sunflower seeds

1 tablespoon chopped almonds

25 g (1 oz) ready-to-eat dried apricots, chopped

2 tablespoons orange or apple juice

2 small eating apples, peeled and grated

3 tablespoons skimmed or soya milk

1 Place the oats, sultanas or raisins, seeds, almonds and apricots in a bowl with the fruit juice.

2 Add the grated apples and stir to mix. Top with your chosen milk and serve.

kcal: **340 (1428 kj)**
protein: **10 g**
carbohydrate: **39 g**
fat: **12 g**
GI: **L**

nutrition tip:
If you're not a morning person, make this muesli the night before. Carry out step 1 and put the mixture in the refrigerator overnight. The next morning, add the apples and milk. This will also give a softer-textured muesli.

day 4

You are halfway through your first week and your insulin levels will be starting to level out. Your body will have started to burn fat for fuel – and you will have lost at least 0.25 kg (½ lb). Don't get on the scales yet though – instead, just focus on the fact that every day from now means more weight lost.

breakfast

bowl of noodle-shaped bran cereal
50 g (2 oz), topped with 150 ml (¼ pint) skimmed or soya milk and 1 sliced banana

glass of unsweetened grapefruit juice
150 ml (¼ pint)

snack

small tub of tzatziki
125 g (4 oz), served with 4 celery sticks

lunch

Herby Lentil Salad with Bacon
(see recipe, right)

ALTERNATIVE:
quick lentil salad
Mix 200 g (7 oz) rinsed and drained canned lentils with 75 g (3 oz) of lean ham, 3 chopped spring onions, 1 tablespoon of chopped parsley, a squeeze of lemon juice and season to taste

snack

blueberry smoothie
made from 150 ml (¼ pint) soya milk, 150 g (5 oz) soya yogurt and 100 g (3½ oz) blueberries

dinner

scallops with pasta
Pan-fry 8–10 queen scallops per person in a little lemon juice and oil from an oil spray. Serve with 50 g (2 oz) of pasta spirals per person, on a bed of mixed salad leaves, sliced tomato, red pepper and cucumber

ALTERNATIVE:
prawns with pasta
If you can't find scallops, use 150 g (5 oz) prawns per person, cooked in a little lemon juice and garlic

circuit **training**

Do a little circuit training – this works all the muscles of your body and the variety stops you getting bored or too tired. A simple circuit would be 1 minute each of jogging on the spot, star jumps, skipping, stair climbing and sprinting between two points. Do the workout in your garden, the park or even in the house and repeat as many times as you like.

Calories burnt: 50 per circuit

herby lentil salad with bacon

preparation time: 10 minutes

cooking time: 5 minutes

serves 4

oil spray (see tip, right)

1 garlic clove, crushed

4 spring onions, sliced

2 x 400 g (13 oz) cans green lentils, drained and rinsed

2 tablespoons balsamic vinegar

3 tablespoons chopped herbs (such as parsley, oregano or basil)

125 g (4 oz) cherry tomatoes, halved

85 g (3¼ oz) back bacon rashers, sliced

1 Spray a nonstick pan with oil, add the garlic and spring onions and fry for 2 minutes.

2 Stir in the lentils, vinegar, herbs and tomatoes and set aside (or if you're taking this to work, put in an airtight container until you want to eat it).

did you know?

We are only aware of 30 per cent of the sugar that we eat – the other 70 per cent is hidden in processed foods. Always read labels carefully and choose brands with no sugar, or those where it appears towards the end of the ingredients list.

3 Grill the bacon until crisp, place on top of the salad and serve. If you're eating at work, wrap the cooked, crisped bacon in kitchen paper, then kitchen foil. Add just before you eat.

kcal: **313 (1314 kj)**
protein: **24 g**
carbohydrate: **27 g**
fat: **12 g**
GI: **L**

nutrition tip:
Today you have two recipes using an oil spray. Get a spray bottle from a kitchen shop and half fill with olive oil, then top up with water. Every time a recipe calls for oil to moisten a pan for frying, spritz with this to save calories.

day 5

You should be appreciating the fill-up factor of this eating plan by now – and not experiencing the hunger pangs or sugar cravings you get on a normal weight-loss diet. If it weren't for your clothes feeling looser, you could almost forget you were dieting.

breakfast

omelette
made from 1 whole egg and 3 egg whites. Fill with 50 g (2 oz) grated low-fat Cheddar cheese. Serve with 1 grilled tomato

glass of any unsweetened fruit juice
150 ml (¼ pint)

ALTERNATIVE:
cold platter
25 g (1 oz) lean ham, 25 g (1 oz) cheese, 1 sliced tomato, 1 slice of dark rye bread with wholegrains (or granary, soya or barley bread)

glass of any unsweetened orange or apple juice
150 ml (¼ pint)

snack

1 pear or apple

25 g (1 oz) pumpkin seeds

lunch

Tabbouleh Salad
(see recipe, right), served with 100 g (3½ oz) sliced cooked chicken

snack

2 rye crispbreads
spread with 50 g (2 oz) low-fat pâté

green grapes
50 g (2 oz)

dinner

cod in parsley sauce
Melt a teaspoon of butter in a pan with 2 tablespoons of white wine. Poach a 75 g (3 oz) cod steak in the pan with a tablespoon of chopped parsley. Season and serve with 50 g (2 oz) quinoa or buckwheat, cooked according to packet instructions, and unlimited carrots, broccoli and kale

mental **workout**

Give the hardcore exercise a rest today, and do some yoga instead. Either join a yoga class or rent a yoga video from a video store. Not only will it help lengthen your muscles, it will also still your mind – good news, as stress increases levels of fat-storing hormones in the system.

Calories burnt: 150–600 per hour

tabbouleh salad

preparation time: 15 minutes, plus standing

serves 4

175 g (6 oz) bulgar wheat

300 ml (½ pint) boiling water

1 red onion, finely chopped

3 tomatoes, diced

½ cucumber, chopped

10 tablespoons chopped parsley

5 tablespoons chopped mint

DRESSING

100 ml (3½ fl oz) lemon juice

2 teaspoons olive oil

freshly ground black pepper

1 Place the bulgar wheat in a bowl. Pour over the boiling water and leave to stand for 30 minutes, or according to packet instructions, until the grains swell and soften.

diet **power-up**

Green tea is a great low-GI beverage choice – but as well as this it has been shown to help increase the cells' response to insulin – and boost calorie burning. Four cups a day stokes the metabolic rate by around 4 per cent, leading to an extra 65 calories a day burnt painlessly – that's the equivalent to a 6-minute bicycle ride.

2 Drain the bulgar wheat and press to remove the excess moisture. Place in a salad bowl. Add the onion, tomatoes, cucumber, parsley and mint. Toss to combine.

3 Place all the dressing ingredients in a screw-top jar, replace the lid and shake well to combine. Pour over the salad and toss well.

kcal: **193 (810 kj)**
protein: **5 g**
carbohydrate: **36 g**
fat: **3 g**
GI: **L**

nutrition tip:
Rich in B vitamins, iron, phosphorus and manganese, bulgar is one of the most nutritious of the grains. It also contains heart-protecting vitamin E.

day 6

If you started this diet on a Monday, this will be your first weekend day on the plan – don't let this throw you. You can still enjoy your weekend and stick to your diet – and if you do decide to go out for a meal, don't think you've blown it. Just try to order within the low-GI rules and get back on the plan tomorrow.

breakfast

1 boiled egg with 2 rye crispbreads topped with yeast extract

Serve with half a grapefruit and a smoothie made with ¼ pint (150 ml) skimmed milk and 4 handfuls of blueberries, strawberries or raspberries

snack

1 slice of toast
Choose granary, barley or soya bread and top with 1 tablespoon of peanut butter

lunch

Bean Salad
(see recipe, far right), topped with 100 g (3½ oz) canned tuna in spring water, 8 baby carrots and 5 cherry tomatoes

snack

1 apple or orange

dinner

salmon steak
150 g (5 oz). Serve with 6 asparagus spears sprinkled with 25 g (1 oz) freshly grated Parmesan cheese then grilled until the cheese melts and the asparagus spears slightly char, and 100 g (3½ oz) of new potatoes and 75 g (3 oz) of peas

exercise of the day

Go in-line skating. If the weather's cold – or you don't own blades – try ice-skating instead. Both will tone your bottom, thighs and stomach.

**Calories burnt:
315 in 30 minutes**

buckwheat pancakes

preparation time: 5 minutes, plus standing

cooking time: 25 minutes

serves 4

50 g (2 oz) wholemeal flour

50 g (2 oz) buckwheat flour

1 egg

300 ml (½ pint) skimmed milk

8 teaspoons olive oil

fresh fruit, to serve

1 Sift the flours into a bowl and add the grains left in the sieve. Beat the egg and milk together, then slowly add to the flour. Stir until a smooth batter forms. If the mixture is a little thick, add a little more milk. Leave to stand for 20 minutes, then stir again.

2 Put 1 teaspoon of oil in a nonstick frying pan. When it's hot, add 2 tablespoons of the pancake mixture and shake the pan so it spreads. Cook for 2 minutes until the underside is lightly browned, then turn over and cook the other side for a minute or so.

3 Keep the pancake warm in the oven while you cook the rest, repeating step 2.

kcal: **230 (966 kj)**
protein: **7 g**
carbohydrate: **13 g**
fat: **5 g**
GI: **L**

nutrition tip:
Buckwheat is a major source of the amino acid lysine. Our body cannot make this and relies on getting a supply from food – lysine is vital for calcium absorption, but also to create healthy collagen.

motivation booster

Don't forget that nibbling while you are cooking can sabotage your diet by providing unwanted calories – chew sugar-free gum while you cook to prevent this.

bean salad

preparation time: 10 minutes

cooking time: 3 minutes

serves 1

75 g (3 oz) sliced green beans

50 g (2 oz) canned red kidney beans, rinsed and drained

25 g (1 oz) canned chickpeas, rinsed and drained

¼ onion, finely chopped

1 teaspoon chopped coriander

1 teaspoon olive oil

salt and pepper

1 Cook the green beans in lightly salted boiling water for 3 minutes, then drain and refresh under cold running water.

2 Mix together all the ingredients in a bowl and serve.

kcal: **161 (676 kj)**
protein: **7 g**
carbohydrate: **20 g**
fat: **6 g**
GI: **L**

day 7

Halfway through, so today would be a good day to gauge your progress. Either step on the scales, or use your tape measure to see what you have lost and from where. And remember that losing weight isn't the only benefit you will have achieved by now: think about your improved energy levels and moods.

breakfast

cooked breakfast
2 rashers of back bacon trimmed of all fat, grilled mushroom, grilled tomato, 100 g (3½ oz) of canned baked beans and 1 slice of barley or granary toast

snack

1 orange or 3 satsumas

glass of skimmed or soya milk
150 ml (¼ pint)

lunch

roast lunch
150 g (5 oz) roast chicken, beef or pork (no skin, crackling or other fat). Serve with 2 roast sweet potatoes, unlimited carrots, green beans and Brussels sprouts, and 1 tablespoon of gravy

snack

2 digestive biscuits
spread with a little fruit conserve

dinner

Warm Aubergine Salad
(see recipe, right). Serve with a 150 g (5 oz) sole or cod fillet, grilled or poached, and a large salad of mixed leaves topped with a little low-fat salad dressing, or lemon juice and black pepper

enjoyable exercise

Exercise can be fun. Choose any of the following to burn 150 calories today.

- Play ten-pin bowling for 40 minutes
- Wash the car (by hand) for 37 minutes
- Play pool for 1 hour
- Mow the lawn for 23 minutes
- Walk the dog for 30 minutes
- Play catch for 20 minutes
- Window-shop for 1 hour
- Play table tennis or badminton for 25 minutes

warm aubergine salad

preparation time: 10 minutes, plus cooling

cooking time: 10 minutes

serves 4

2 tablespoons olive oil

2 aubergines, cut into small cubes

1 red onion, finely sliced

2 tablespoons capers, roughly chopped

4 tomatoes, chopped

4 tablespoons chopped parsley

1 tablespoon balsamic vinegar

salt and pepper

1 Heat the oil in a nonstick frying pan (or use your oil spray to cut calories further). Add the aubergines and fry for 10 minutes until golden and softened.

did you know?

Not getting enough sleep makes cells more resistant to insulin and may therefore promote fat storage. This is even more important when you realize that fatigue is one of the top three reasons why many of us reach for sugary or high-fat snacks. Try to get eight hours sleep a night.

2 Add the onion, capers, tomatoes, parsley and vinegar and stir to combine. Season lightly to taste. Remove from the heat and leave to cool for 10 minutes before serving.

kcal: **99 (416 kj)**
protein: **3 g**
carbohydrate: **9 g**
fat: **6 g**
GI: **L**

nutrition tip:
Aubergines are a good source of folic acid and contain cancer-beating antioxidants. They tend to soak up oil, though, so be careful when cooking.

day 8

By now you will have noticed a definite change in your energy levels – you should be waking up feeling alert and not having mid-afternoon or early evening slumps. Use your new-found get-up-and-go to enjoy yourself – the more active you become, the better life is (and the more weight you lose).

breakfast

wake-up smoothie
made from 50 g (2 oz) strawberries, 50 g (2 oz) raspberries, 150 ml (¼ pint) of orange juice and 0.5 cm (¼ inch) sliver of fresh root ginger (peeled). Process in a blender until smooth

2 slices of toast
Choose granary, barley or soya bread and top each with 1 teaspoon of peanut butter

snack

small tub of low-fat hummus
about 125 g (4 oz), with 2 carrots cut into crudités

lunch

cherry tomato and pasta salad
Cook 50 g (2 oz) dried penne, cool and mix with 6 halved cherry tomatoes, ½ yellow pepper, sliced, 25 g (1 oz) of pine nuts and 15 g (½ oz) of grated Parmesan cheese. Add a squeeze of lemon juice, season to taste and serve with watercress

snack

pot of low-fat fruit yogurt
150 g (5 oz)

dinner

Pan-fried Lamb with Spiced Flageolet Beans
(see recipe, right), served with 100 g (3½ oz) of broccoli and mangetout per person

ALTERNATIVE:
grilled lean lamb chop
about 150 g (5 oz), served with 75 g (3 oz) of canned butter beans, 100 g (3½ oz) of broccoli and mangetout and 1 tablespoon of gravy

pushing **harder**

Go for a 30-minute walk, run, swim or bicycle ride. Every 2 minutes, go as fast as you can for 30–60 seconds. Slow for 2 minutes, then do another fast spurt.

Calories burnt:
20 per cent more than normal – 170 for a walk, 260 for a swim and 360 for a run or bicycle ride

pan-fried lamb with spiced flageolet beans

preparation time: 10 minutes, plus marinating

cooking time: 12 minutes

serves 4

½ **teaspoon ground cumin**

½ **teaspoon ground coriander**

pinch of chilli powder

1 tablespoon olive oil

4 lean lamb steaks

1 onion, sliced

1 garlic clove, crushed

4 tablespoons lemon juice

400 g (13 oz) can flageolet beans, drained and rinsed

1 tablespoon chopped mint

2 tablespoons low-fat crème fraîche

1 Mix together the cumin, coriander, chilli and half the oil in a non-metallic bowl. Add the lamb, coat it in the spices and set aside for 10 minutes.

2 Heat the remaining oil in a non-stick pan, add the onion and garlic and fry for 3–4 minutes until softened.

motivation booster

If you can't summon up the energy to do your workout, take a sniff of peppermint oil, or eat a mint before you start. Research shows that exercisers run faster, do more sit-ups and feel stronger after inhaling the smell of mint.

3 Add the lamb and the marinade and fry the steaks for 2–3 minutes on each side – or until cooked to your liking.

4 Add the lemon juice, flageolet beans, mint and crème fraîche and simmer for 1 minute until warmed through.

kcal: **261 (1096 kj)**
protein: **26 g**
carbohydrate: **16 g**
fat: **12 g**
GI: **L**

nutrition tip:
Flageolet beans are often described as the caviar of beans. They are tiny green members of the haricot family and, like most beans, contain high levels of B vitamins, iron and potassium.

day 9

By now your clothes should be feeling slightly looser around the waist, hips or thighs – and if you've been exercising regularly you should also have started to notice some firming of your legs, bottom and tummy muscles. Really focus on the gains you are making and remember that each day you carry on means more benefits to your body.

breakfast

scrambled eggs
made from 2 eggs, a splash of milk and a dab of butter. Serve on 1 slice of granary, soya or barley toast

snack

2 kiwi fruit or 2 handfuls of cherries

lunch

crab and avocado burrito
Spread 1 wholemeal tortilla wrap with a little salsa. Fill with 50 g (2 oz) of crab meat (fresh or canned) and ½ avocado, sliced. Wrap up and serve with 200 g (7 oz) of canned red kidney beans, mixed with a little crushed garlic, chilli powder, lemon juice and olive oil

snack

protein shake
(see page 42)

dinner

Spicy Lentil and Tomato Soup
(see recipe, right), served with a 100 g (3½ oz) chunk of granary, barley or soya bread

ALTERNATIVE:
carton of lentil, minestrone or vegetable soup
400 g (13 oz), served with bread, as above

going **backwards**

Gym workouts can get dull – today, try the treadmill backwards. Holding onto the handrails, walk or run backwards for up to 5 minutes – it burns up to 32 per cent more calories than going forwards, as you take more steps. If you don't feel safe on the treadmill, try it on the ground first.

spicy lentil and tomato soup

preparation time: 10–15 minutes

cooking time: 40–50 minutes

serves 4

250 g (8 oz) red lentils

1 tablespoon vegetable oil

1 large onion, finely chopped

1 garlic clove, finely chopped

1 celery stick, finely chopped

200 g (7 oz) can chopped tomatoes, drained

½ small green chilli, deseeded and finely chopped (optional)

½ teaspoon paprika

½ teaspoon harissa paste

½ teaspoon ground cumin

600 ml (1 pint) vegetable stock or water

salt and pepper

1 tablespoon chopped coriander, to garnish

1 Place the lentils in a bowl of water. Heat the oil in a large saucepan and gently fry the onion, garlic and celery over a low heat until softened.

2 Drain the lentils and add them to the vegetable pan with the tomatoes. Mix well. Add the chilli, if using, paprika, harissa paste, cumin and vegetable stock and season with salt and pepper. Cover the pan and simmer gently for about 30–40 minutes, until the lentils are soft, adding a little more vegetable stock or water if the soup gets too thick.

3 Serve the soup immediately in warmed individual bowls topped with a little chopped coriander.

kcal: **288 (1210 kj)**
protein: **18 g**
carbohydrate: **28 g**
fat: **2 g**
GI: **L**

nutrition tip:
Soups are great diet foods as the combination of fluid and fibre fills you up. This one works well as it contains lentils, which are particularly filling, and metabolism-boosting chillies.

diet **power-up**

Are you drinking enough water? Being dehydrated not only gives you thirst cravings that many of us mistake for hunger, it also slows your metabolism. You will burn 2–3 per cent more calories if you are properly hydrated.

day 10

Did you realize that so far following this diet plan you've eaten more fruit and vegetables than the average person eats in 10 weeks? Therefore, as well as all the health-boosting effects of a low-GI diet, you are also harnessing all the power of the nutrients and antioxidants found in fresh fruit and vegetables – no wonder you look and feel better already.

breakfast

bowl of porridge
(see page 40). Add 25 g (1 oz) of sultanas and ½ apple, finely chopped, and mix well

glass of unsweetened orange or grapefruit juice
150 ml (¼ pint)

snack

1 slice of granary, soya or barley bread
topped with 25 g (1 oz) tuna in spring water

lunch

prawn coleslaw
Mix 100 g (3½ oz) of peeled prawns with 1 tablespoon reduced-fat mayonnaise and unlimited shredded white cabbage, carrot and red onion. Serve with 1 small wholemeal pitta bread

snack

10 olives

5 almonds

dinner

Gammon Steaks with Creamy Lentils
(see recipe, right), served with broccoli and green beans

ALTERNATIVE:
grilled gammon steak
150 g (5 oz), served with 75 g (3 oz) of canned lentils tossed with a squeeze of lemon juice and some chopped herbs, and unlimited green vegetables

be a **water baby**

It doesn't matter what stroke you do, just aim to do 30 minutes of swimming today. You burn as many calories swimming a fast front crawl as you would running, but it feels easier as your body doesn't have to fight against gravity.

Calories burnt: 200–360

gammon steaks with creamy lentils

preparation time: 8 minutes

cooking time: 25–30 minutes

serves 4

125 g (4 oz) Puy lentils

50 g (2 oz) butter

2 shallots

1 garlic clove, chopped

2 thyme sprigs, crushed

1 teaspoon cumin seeds

4 teaspoons Dijon mustard

2 teaspoons clear honey

4 gammon steaks, 150 g (5 oz) each

125 ml (4 fl oz) dry cider

75 ml (3 fl oz) single cream

salt and pepper

1 Place the lentils in a pan and cover with cold water. Bring to the boil and cook for 20 minutes.

2 Meanwhile, melt the butter in a frying pan and fry the shallots, garlic, thyme and cumin seeds, stirring frequently, for 10 minutes until the shallots are soft and golden.

3 Blend the mustard and honey and season to taste with salt and pepper. Brush the mixture over the gammon steaks and grill for 3 minutes on each side until golden and cooked through. Keep warm.

4 Drain the lentils and add them to the shallot mixture. Pour in the cider, bring to the boil and cook until reduced to about 4 tablespoons. Stir in the cream, heat through and season to taste with salt and pepper. Serve with the gammon steaks, garnished with thyme leaves.

kcal: **420 (1764 kj)**
protein: **22 g**
carbohydrate: **35 g**
fat: **21 g**
GI: **L**

nutrition tip:
Gammon contains the same amount of fat as a skinless chicken breast and is therefore a healthy eating choice – so long as you remember to cut the fat off on the side and choose unsalted brands. It is also high in energy-giving B vitamins and contains low levels of iron.

did you know?

People who eat a low-GI diet have lower blood pressure than those eating the high-GI way.

day 11

You may be noticing more beneficial effects of the GI diet by now. Those prone to skin breakouts may have found them less severe. And by avoiding the sugars that cause inflammation, your skin may look smoother and younger. On top of this, the fact that you are getting protein from a variety of sources, and plenty of calcium, means your hair and nails are benefiting too.

breakfast

cottage cheese and fruit
100 g (3½ oz) of low-fat cottage cheese mixed with 1 sliced banana, 1 sliced pear, a handful of berries and ½ mango. Serve with 1 slice of fruit bread, toasted

snack

2 rye crispbreads
topped with 1 teaspoon of hummus and 1 sliced tomato

lunch

chicken caesar salad
125 g (4 oz) of grilled chicken and unlimited iceberg lettuce mixed with 1 tablespoon of low-fat caesar salad dressing, topped with 15 g (½ oz) grated Parmesan

can or carton of minestrone, tomato or lentil soup
400 g (13 oz)

snack

2 satsumas

dinner

Teriyaki Salmon on Noodles
(see recipe, right), served with unlimited steamed bok choy

ALTERNATIVE:
grilled salmon steak
175 g (6 oz), served with 50 g (2 oz) of dry egg noodles, cooked according to packet instructions, unlimited bok choy, and 1 teaspoon of sweet chilli sauce

learn something **new**

Try a different exercise class: great calorie-burners are Step, Spinning or Kickboxing classes, while Pump, Pilates or Sculpt classes are good body-toners. If you can't get out, hire an exercise video: salsa, martial arts, Tae Bo or general aerobics tapes need no special equipment.

Calories burnt: 400–600 per hour for calorie burners, 150–300 for toners

teriyaki salmon on noodles

preparation time: 10 minutes, plus marinating

cooking time: 12 minutes

serves 4

4 skinless salmon fillets, about 125 g (4 oz) each

2 tablespoons soy sauce

1 tablespoon dry sherry

2 tablespoons soft brown sugar

2 garlic cloves, crushed

1 teaspoon grated fresh root ginger

1 tablespoon sesame oil

2 tablespoons water

2 tablespoons sesame seeds

2 spring onions, chopped

250 g (8 oz) dried rice noodles, cooked according to packet instructions

3 tablespoons chopped coriander leaves

1 Place the salmon on a foil-lined grill pan. Mix together the soy sauce, sherry, sugar, garlic, ginger, half of the oil and the water. Brush half the marinade over the salmon and set aside for 10 minutes.

diet **power-up**

Never guess your portions when trying to lose weight – we tend to serve double the amount we are supposed to have, adding up to hundreds of calories a day. Always weigh portions – or in restaurants, remember protein shouldn't be bigger than your palm. Carbohydrate portions are half a tennis ball in volume.

2 Cook the salmon under a preheated hot grill for 5–6 minutes, turning it halfway through the cooking time and brushing with a little more of the marinade.

3 Meanwhile, heat the remaining oil in a saucepan, add the sesame seeds and spring onions and fry for 1 minute. Add the noodles and any remaining marinade to the saucepan and heat through. Stir in the coriander. Serve the salmon on a bed of noodles.

kcal: **504 (2117 kJ)**
protein: **30 g**
carbohydrate: **50 g**
fat: **20 g**
GI: **L**

nutritional tip:
Salmon is an excellent source of vitamin E, vitamin A and the essential fatty acids that we need for a healthy body. Tinned salmon also provides calcium in its bones.

day 12

You're on the home stretch and by now your body should really start to be regaining control of its insulin levels. As a result, it's time for a treat. Whichever treat you choose this afternoon, make sure you really enjoy it.

breakfast

Walnut and Banana Sunrise Smoothie
(see recipe, right)

bowl of cereal
25 g (1 oz) noodle-shaped bran cereal, topped with 150 ml (¼ pint) of skimmed milk and 50 g (2 oz) of berries

ALTERNATIVE:
glass of unsweetened orange, grapefruit or cranberry juice
150 ml (¼ pint)

bowl of cereal
25 g (1 oz) noodle-shaped bran cereal topped with 150 ml (¼ pint) of skimmed milk, 50 g (2 oz) of berries and 15 g (½ oz) of chopped walnuts

snack

small tub of tzatziki
125 g (4 oz), served with 2 carrots cut into crudités

lunch

open sandwich
made from 1 slice of granary, barley or soya bread spread with a little mustard and topped with 50 g (2 oz) of ham, and 50 g (2 oz) of cooked sliced chicken or turkey. Add sliced tomatoes, cucumber and lettuce or alfalfa sprouts

Bean Salad
(see recipe, page 51), 100 g (3½ oz)

snack

sweet treat
choose from: a 30 g (1 oz) bar of plain or milk chocolate, 2 scoops of any low-fat ice cream or frozen yogurt, or 2 chocolate biscuits

dinner

steak or sole
150 g (5 oz) sirloin steak or sole fillet, grilled and served with 75 g (3 oz) of roasted, mashed or chipped sweet potatoes and 75 g (3 oz) of peas

do some weights

For today's exercise, go to the gym and use the weights – if you don't know how, ask an instructor to show you. Weight training not only tones your body, it also helps build muscle that burns calories even when you sit still.

Calories burnt:
150 in 30 minutes

walnut and banana sunrise smoothie

preparation time: 10 minutes

serves 2

1 orange, segmented

1 banana

150 ml (¼ pint) soya or skimmed milk

150 g (5 oz) soya or natural yogurt

25 g (1 oz) walnut pieces

1 teaspoon clear honey

1 Place all the ingredients in a food processor or blender and blend until smooth and frothy. Pour into two glasses and serve.

kcal: **265 (1113 kj)** *(skimmed milk)*, **273 (1146 kj)** *(soya milk)*
protein: **10 g**
carbohydrate: **35 g** *(skimmed milk)*, **30 g** *(soya milk)*
fat: **11 g** *(skimmed milk)*, **13 g** *(soya milk)*
GI: **L**

nutrition tip:
Soya is a good source of nutrients called phytoestrogens which have been shown to balance hormone levels. They may reduce the risk of breast cancer in women and also make menopausal symptoms more manageable.

day 13

You could be surprised that this morning starts with a full cooked breakfast – but everything in this meal is a low-GI food, meaning you can eat it and still lose weight. Use it to power up another active weekend.

breakfast

cooked breakfast
1 boiled or poached egg, 1 rasher of lean back bacon or one low-fat sausage grilled well, 125 g (4 oz) of canned baked beans and 3 grilled mushrooms

glass of unsweetened orange juice
150 ml (¼ pint)

snack

100 g (3½ oz) strawberries

lunch

falafel salad
6 grilled falafel balls, served with a large salad of rocket, bean sprouts, tomato, green pepper and ½ avocado

snack

cheese and grapes
50 g (2 oz) Edam or low-fat Cheddar and 100 g (3½ oz) red grapes

dinner

Griddled Chicken with Pearl Barley
(see recipe, right)

ALTERNATIVE:
grilled chicken with pasta
150 g (5 oz) grilled chicken breast, served with 50 g (2 oz) of dried pasta spirals or 50 g (2 oz) of dried lentils, cooked according to packet instructions, and a large mixed salad

get **adventurous**

If there's an indoor (or outdoor) ski slope near you, strap on some skis. If there's a rock climbing wall, then go and climb it. Or try your first horse ride. While you are learning something new, it won't feel like exercise.

Calories burnt: 400–600 per hour

griddled chicken with pearl barley

preparation time: 50 minutes

cooking time: 10 minutes

serves 4

4 boneless, skinless chicken breasts

1 tablespoon olive oil

125 g (4 oz) pearl barley, cooked according to packet instructions

1 red onion, finely chopped

1 red chilli, finely chopped

4 tablespoons chopped coriander leaves

grated rind and juice of 2 limes

1 red pepper, cored, deseeded and finely chopped

salt and pepper

TO GARNISH

chopped parsley

lime wedges

1 Brush each chicken piece with a little oil. Heat a griddle pan until hot and cook the chicken for 4–5 minutes on each side until golden and cooked through. Cut each breast into 4 slices.

diet **power-up**

Fidget – tapping your fingers, swinging a leg, running up and down to get things all burn calories, to the extent that fidgeters burn 800 calories a day more than those who sit still, according to researchers at the Mayo Clinic in the USA. Make it rule never to sit completely still.

2 Stir the remaining oil into the barley and add the onion, chilli, coriander, lime rind and juice and red pepper. Season to taste with salt and pepper and stir to combine.

3 Serve the barley topped with the chicken, garnished with parsley and lime wedges.

kcal: **360 (1512 kj)**
protein: **40 g**
carbohydrate: **30 g**
fat: **10 g**
GI: **L**

nutrition tip
Pearl barley may take a long time to cook, but it's worth it for the nutritional benefits. It is an excellent source of soluble fibre and can actually help lower cholesterol levels. Plus, barley contains B vitamins, iron and other essential vitamins.

day 14

This is the end of your organized plan – get on the scales, or grab a tape measure and see how you have done. But just because the plan is over, it doesn't mean your weight loss efforts have to be – you can either repeat the programme as many times as it takes to get to your desired weight, or use the low-GI rules to create your own plan.

breakfast

Buckwheat Pancakes
(see recipe, page 51), served with 1 sliced banana and 1 teaspoon of maple syrup

glass of soya or skimmed milk
150 ml (¼ pint)

snack

25 g (1 oz) almonds

50 g (2 oz) raspberries

lunch

salmon salad
100 g (3½ oz) of canned salmon or tuna in spring water, drained and served with a large green salad and 75 g (3 oz) of boiled new potatoes

snack

pot of low-fat yogurt or fromage frais
150 g (5 oz)

dinner

Vegetable Curry
(see recipe, right), served with 25 g (1 oz) of dried basmati rice and 50 g (2 oz) of dried lentils, cooked according to packet instructions, plus a serving of spinach sprinkled with a little lemon juice and nutmeg

ALTERNATIVE:
ready-made vegetable curry
Choose one with under 300 kcal (1260 kj). Serve with rice, lentils and spinach, as above

get **competitive**

Play your partner or a friend at a one-on-one sport like tennis, squash or badminton.

Calories burnt: 300 per 30-minute game

vegetable curry

preparation time: 10 minutes

cooking time: 25 minutes

serves 4

1 tablespoon olive oil

1 onion, chopped

1 garlic clove, crushed

2 tablespoons medium curry paste

1.5 kg (3 lb) prepared vegetables (such as courgettes, peppers, squash, mushrooms and green beans)

200 g (7 oz) can chopped tomatoes

400 g (13 oz) can reduced-fat coconut milk

2 tablespoons chopped coriander leaves

1 Heat the oil in a large saucepan (or use your oil spray as before), add the onion and garlic and fry for 2 minutes, Stir in the curry paste and fry for 1 minute more.

did you know?

Sunlight actually helps the brain create serotonin and may help reduce the amount of carbohydrates you crave. If you're missing any favourite foods, try and get outside today to boost your health, and your weight loss.

2 Add the vegetables and fry for 2–3 minutes, stirring occasionally, then add the tomatoes and coconut milk. Stir well, bring to the boil then lower the heat and simmer for 12–15 minutes or until all the vegetables are cooked. Stir in the coriander and serve.

kcal: **268 (1125 kj)**
protein: **6 g**
carbohydrate: **35 g**
fat: **11 g**
GI: **L**

nutritional tip:
Coconut milk contains saturated fat so you shouldn't eat it every day, but it does give a great flavour to curries. Just choose reduced-fat versions – and remember, some studies show coconut milk can boost the immune system.

VEGETARIAN WEIGHT-LOSS PLAN

This diet plan has been specially devised for vegetarians. With delicious recipes and meal suggestions, it means you won't have to compromise on flavour either.

You will see that much of this plan is the same as the Genius Weight-Loss Plan – that is because the emphasis on grains, fruit and vegetables means much of it is suitable for vegetarians anyway. All the suggestions for exercise and motivation boosters apply to both plans, so it's a good idea to read the Genius Weight-Loss Plan even if you aren't a meat eater.

day 1

This is it – the first day on your path to a healthy, slim figure. Before you start, take a few minutes to look at yourself in the mirror and focus on what you like about your body. Studies show that this doubles your chances of sticking to any weight-loss plan.

breakfast

bowl of porridge
Use 75 g (3 oz) rolled oats and make according to packet instructions. Top with a large handful of blueberries, strawberries or sliced peaches instead of sugar

glass of unsweetened orange juice
150 ml (¼ pint)

snack

pot of low-fat fruit yogurt
150 g (5 oz)

handful of dried apricots
50 g (2 oz)

lunch

Moroccan Tomato and Chickpea Salad
(see recipe, page 41), served with 2 slices of granary, soya or barley bread spread with 2 tablespoons hummus

ALTERNATIVE:
quick bean salad
Mix 200 g (7 oz) of canned mixed beans with a squeeze of lemon juice, a teaspoon of olive oil, half a red onion, finely chopped, and a handful of herbs such as parsley and basil. Serve with bread and hummus, as above, and a large salad of lettuce, cucumber and tomato

snack

1 banana

5 brazil nuts

dinner

grilled Quorn™ steak
topped with 1 tablespoon of Tomato and Pepper Salsa (see recipe, page 41), 100 g (3½ oz) of new potatoes and 75 g (3 oz) of mangetout

did you know?

The commonest cause of fatigue is lack of iron. You can help build stores by drinking a small glass of orange juice with meals that include green vegetables – this helps boost iron absorption.

day 2

On day 2 it's good to look at what went well on the first day – and what didn't. Knowing where you might slip up in the future will help you to succeed for the rest of the plan, so spend a few minutes thinking about what will help you to stick to it today.

breakfast

Pumpkin Seed and Apricot Muesli
(see recipe, page 45)

glass of unsweetened grapefruit juice
150 ml (¼ pint)

ALTERNATIVE:
muesli
50 g (2 oz) of any unsweetened muesli, topped with 150 ml (¼ pint) of skimmed or soya milk

½ grapefruit

snack

½ mango
topped with 50 g (2 oz) low-fat cottage cheese

lunch

open sandwich
made from 1 slice of granary, barley or soya bread, and 50 g (2 oz) of grated cheese, or ½ avocado, sliced. Top with 1 sliced tomato and a handful of alfalfa sprouts

can or carton of lentil soup
400 g (13 oz)

snack

15 olives

dinner

spaghetti bolognese
made from 75 g (3 oz) of soya mince per person and a jar of ready-made tomato pasta sauce. Serve with 50 g (2 oz) of dried pasta per person, cooked according to packet instructions

diet **power-up**

If you follow a regular exercise programme, you need to change it a little every 6 weeks or it won't work so well. Use the exercise tips to give you some new ideas.

day 3

You may only be a few days into your diet but already you'll start to notice positive improvements in your mood and energy levels as you stabilize blood sugar levels and prevent falls and crashes that lead to fatigue and irritation.

breakfast

glass of unsweetened orange juice
150 ml (¼ pint)

2 slices of toast
Choose granary, barley or soya bread and spread with 2 teaspoons of ricotta cheese and 2 teaspoons of all-fruit conserve

1 apple

snack

protein shake
made from 2 scoops of whey protein powder mixed with water, and 100 g (3½ oz) tinned peaches in natural juice. Whey protein is a great low-fat, low-GI drink that can be found in health food stores and some supermarkets

ALTERNATIVE:
pot of low-fat fruit yogurt
150 g (5 oz)

lunch

small tub of low-fat hummus
about 125 g (4 oz), served with 3 rye crispbreads and crudités of carrot, cucumber, celery and cherry tomatoes

snack

handful of white grapes
50 g (2 oz)

did you know?

We are only aware of 30% of the sugar we eat. The other 70% comes hidden in processed foods, so read labels carefully and choose brands with no sugar or those where it appears at the end of the ingredients list.

dinner

Stuffed Red Onions
(see recipe, right), served with 25 g (1 oz) of dried couscous, prepared according to packet instructions, and a mixed leaf salad drizzled with balsamic vinegar

ALTERNATIVE:
bulgar and roasted vegetables
75 g (3 oz) dried bulgar wheat, cooked according to packet instructions, topped with roasted aubergine, courgette, pepper and red onions. Sprinkle with lemon juice and chopped herbs

stuffed red onions

preparation time: 30 minutes

cooking time: 1½ hours

serves 4

4 large red onions, peeled

2 tablespoons olive oil

125 g (4 oz) button mushrooms, finely chopped

75 g (3 oz) bulgar wheat

1 tablespoon chopped parsley

300 ml (½ pint) water

1 tablespoon sultanas

1 tablespoon freshly grated Parmesan (optional)

salt and pepper

1 Cut the top off each onion and scoop out the centre using a teaspoon. Finely chop the scooped-out onion, then fry with the oil in a frying pan until soft and golden brown. Add the mushrooms and stir for a further 5 minutes.

2 Meanwhile, bring a large pan of water to the boil. Add the onion cups and simmer for 10 minutes, or until they begin to soften. Drain well.

3 Add the bulgar, parsley, salt, pepper and water to the mushrooms. Boil for 5 minutes. Cover the pan and simmer for a further 30 minutes or until the grains have softened. Add extra water if needed.

4 Stir the sultanas into the bulgar mixture and spoon into the onions.

5 Put the onions in a roasting tin and cover with foil. Cook in a preheated oven at 190°C (375°F), Gas Mark 5, for 30 minutes. Remove the foil, sprinkle on the Parmesan, cook for a further 10 minutes and serve.

kcal: **184 (772 kj)**
protein: **4 g**
carbohydrate: **35 g**
fat: **9 g**
GI: **L**

nutrition tip:
Red onions are members of the powerful purple foods family (alongside blueberries, red grapes and so on), believed to contain the highest levels of antioxidants.

day 4

If you have been suffering from sugar cravings, the good news is that they'll now start to subside as your brain realises that you're moving away from sweet treats. Don't give in to temptation and you'll stay sugar free.

breakfast

bowl of noodle-shaped bran cereal
50 g (2 oz), topped with 150 ml (¼ pint) skimmed or soya milk

glass of unsweetened grapefruit juice
150 ml (¼ pint)

snack

2 satsumas or 2 kiwi fruit

lunch

Herby Lentil Salad
(see recipe, page 47), replacing the real bacon with 2 vegetarian bacon strips or 40 g (1½ oz) of mozzarella

snack

1 pear or apple

dinner

Brazil Nut and Sunflower Seed Savoury Cakes
(see recipe, right), served with 3 oz (75 g) of steamed asparagus and 2 tablespoons of Tomato and Pepper Salsa (see recipe, page 41).

ALTERNATIVE:
falafel and couscous
6–8 falafel balls, served on 50 g (2 oz) of dried couscous, prepared according to packet instructions, with 5 steamed asparagus spears and 2 tablespoons of Tomato and Pepper Salsa (see recipe, page 41)

diet **power-up**

If you're eating with others serve yourself first, as research shows that we eat more when dining with others than when we eat alone. Another overeating trigger is dimly lit rooms – so swap those candles for bright lights!

brazil nut and sunflower seed savoury cakes

preparation time: 25 minutes, plus chilling

cooking time: 20 minutes

serves 4

250 g (8 oz) brazil nuts, roughly chopped

2 x 425 g (14 oz) cans chickpeas, drained

25 g (1 oz) sunflower seeds

1 tablespoon chopped parsley

1 small onion, finely chopped

2 eggs

125 g (4 oz) soya breadcrumbs

groundnut oil, for brushing

salt and pepper

1 Put the brazil nuts in a blender with the chickpeas. Blend into a smooth mixture. Turn into a bowl, add the sunflower seeds, parsley and onion and mix well.

2 Beat one of the eggs with some salt and pepper. Add to the chickpea mixture and mix well to combine.

3 Take a handful of the mixture, form into a patty and place on a lightly greased baking sheet. Repeat with the rest of the mixture to make 8 large, or 16 small patties.

4 Beat the remaining egg, dip each patty into it, then coat in the breadcrumbs. Chill for 4 hours or overnight.

5 Brush the patties with a little oil and bake in a preheated oven at 200°C (400°F), Gas Mark 6 for 20 minutes, turning once.

kcal: **810 (3402 kj)**
protein: **31 g**
carbohydrate: **46 g**
fat: **55 g**
GI: **L**

nutrition tip:
Brazil nuts are one of the best sources of the essential mineral selenium. This is vital for the healthy function of our immune system and metabolism. They are, however, very high in calories and fat so, if you're snacking on them, watch portions carefully.

day 5

If you eat out it can often seem impossible to stick to the plan. However, most menus will have low-GI options if you look carefully. A few extra calories won't break your diet as long as it only happens occasionally.

breakfast

scrambled eggs
2 scrambled eggs served on 1 slice of granary, barley or soya toast

glass of any unsweetened fruit juice
150 ml (¼ pint)

snack

1 pear or apple

1 tablespoon pumpkin seeds

lunch

Tabbouleh Salad
(see recipe, page 49) served with 1 wholemeal pitta bread

snack

2 rye crispbreads
spread with 50 g (2 oz) of low-fat vegetarian pâté

dinner

Quorn™ steak
served with 100 g (3½ oz) of new potatoes and 50 g (2 oz) of green beans

motivation tip

Cravings shouldn't happen on the GI plan as insulin levels are balanced. If they do, it's the brain talking not the body, so try to distract it.

day 6

If you started this diet on Monday, this will be your first weekend – and a great time to get active. If you haven't looked at the exercise tips in the general weight-loss plan, flick back there now for some ideas of how to build fun activities into your weekend – and boost your weight loss even further.

breakfast

cooked breakfast
2 poached eggs or 200 g (7 oz) of canned baked beans on 2 slices of granary, soya or barley toast

snack

50 g (2 oz) dried apricots

glass of unsweetened fruit juice
150 ml (¼ pint)

lunch

grilled mushrooms
Trim 2 large portobello mushrooms, top with 25 g (1 oz) grated vegetarian cheese and some chopped spring onions and grill until bubbling. Serve with 3 sweet potatoes, roasted or mashed, and 50 g (2 oz) of peas

snack

2 digestive biscuits
spread with a little fruit conserve

1 pear

dinner

Warm Aubergine Salad
(see recipe, page 53). Serve with 50 g (2 oz) of mozzarella and a large salad of mixed leaves topped with a little low-fat salad dressing, or lemon juice and black pepper

diet **power-up**

Are you drinking enough water? Being dehydrated slows your metabolism. You'll burn 2–3% more calories if you're properly hydrated today and every day.

day 7

You have reached half way – which makes it a great time to get on the scales or get out your tape measure to see how you are doing. You should also notice how much your energy, mood and stamina have improved.

breakfast

Buckwheat Pancakes
(see recipe, page 51), topped with 50 g (2 oz) of raspberries and 3 tablespoons of low-fat crème fraîche

glass of carrot juice
150 ml (¼ pint)

ALTERNATIVE:
2 slices of fruit bread
spread with a little low-fat spread and topped with 2 tablespoons of low-fat crème fraîche and 50 g (2 oz) raspberries

snack

1 banana

glass of skimmed milk
150 ml (¼ pint)

lunch

can or carton of lentil, bean or tomato soup
400 g (13 oz), served with 2 slices of granary, barley or soya bread topped with 50 g (2 oz) of grated vegetarian cheese and 1 sliced tomato, toasted

snack

25 peanuts or cashews

motivation tip

Worried that you've only lost a little weight? Pick up something heavy like a 1 kg (2.2 lb) dumbbell and you'll realise just how much 'a little weight' is!

dinner

Lemon Grass and Tofu Nuggets
(see recipe, right), served with 1 teaspoon of sweet chilli sauce and a large salad of rocket, bean sprouts, grated carrot and ½ avocado

ALTERNATIVE:
6–8 vegetarian nuggets
served with chilli sauce and salad, as above

lemon grass and tofu nuggets

preparation time: 10 minutes

cooking time: 4–6 minutes

serves 2

4 spring onions, roughly chopped

2.5 cm (1 inch) piece of fresh root ginger, peeled and chopped

1 lemon grass stalk, finely chopped

3 tablespoons chopped coriander

2 garlic cloves, roughly chopped

½ tablespoon light soy sauce

150 g (5 oz) tofu, drained

40 g (1½ oz) breadcrumbs

1 egg

1 tablespoon olive oil, for brushing

pepper

1 Place the spring onions, ginger, lemon grass, coriander and garlic in a food processor and process lightly until mixed together and chopped, but still quite chunky.

2 Add the soy sauce, tofu, breadcrumbs, egg and pepper and process until just combined.

3 Take dessertspoonfuls of the mixture and pat into flat cakes, using wet hands. Place on a lightly greased grill pan, brush with a little oil and grill under a preheated hot grill for 2–3 minutes on each side until golden.

kcal: **223 (937 kj)**
protein: **14 g**
carbohydrate: **10 g**
fat: **15 g**
GI: **L**

nutrition tip:
Tofu is made from pulverized soya beans, making it a great source of hormone-balancing phytoestrogens. If you don't commonly use tofu in recipes, silken tofu (which is soft) works best in soups or can be eaten raw, firm tofu is better for cooking.

day 8

Yesterday you measured the physical benefits of the plan – today look at the emotional benefits. Have your energy levels improved? Ask friends and family if they have noticed any changes in your mood. The more positive changes you can identify, the easier it will be to stay focused.

breakfast

bowl of porridge
(see page 40). Add 25 g (1 oz) of sultanas and ½ apple, finely chopped, and mix well

glass of unsweetened orange or grapefruit juice
150 ml (¼ pint)

snack

1 slice of granary, soya or barley bread
topped with 25 g (1 oz) of low-fat cottage cheese

lunch

stuffed pitta and coleslaw
1 small wholemeal pitta bread, stuffed with 50 g (2 oz) of vegetarian pâté. Serve with coleslaw made from unlimited shredded white cabbage, carrot and red onion, mixed with 1 tablespoon of low-calorie mayonnaise or vinaigrette

snack

25 g (1 oz) dried apricots

5 almonds

dinner

Baked Buckwheat and Spiced Butter
(see recipe, right), served with 75 g (3 oz) of Brussels sprouts

ALTERNATIVE:
ready-meal vegetable moussaka
Choose one under 400 kcal (1680 kj) and serve with a large green salad, sprinkled with lemon juice and balsamic vinegar

motivation tip

Finding it hard to exercise? Try buying a pedometer and aim to increase your steps by 100 a day. Take the long route to work, pace up and down when you're on the phone and so on. If you can reach 10,000 paces, you've done the equivalent of a 5-mile walk.

baked buckwheat and spiced butter

preparation time: 10 minutes, plus standing

cooking time: 15 minutes

serves 4

75 g (3 oz) unsalted butter, softened

1 small garlic clove, crushed

2 tablespoons chopped fresh coriander

½ teaspoon ground cumin

½ teaspoon ground cinnamon

pinch of chilli powder

250 g (8 oz) roasted buckwheat (kasha)

450 ml (¾ pint) boiling vegetable stock

salt

1 In a small bowl, beat together the butter, garlic, coriander and spices until evenly combined. Cover and leave for at least 30 minutes.

2 Use a little of the spiced butter to grease an ovenproof dish. Put in the roasted buckwheat and pour over the boiling stock. Cover the dish with a tight-fitting lid and place in a preheated oven at 200°C (400°F), Gas Mark 6, for 15 minutes.

3 Remove the dish from the oven and leave to stand for 5 minutes. Stir in the remaining spiced butter, season with salt to taste, and serve at once.

kcal: **375 (1575 kj)**
protein: **6 g**
carbohydrate: **53 g**
fat: **17 g**
GI: **L**

nutrition tip:
Garlic is a good fat-burning food. When we cut calories, our bodies draw fat first from areas with good circulation – and garlic helps boost circulation throughout the whole body. It also contains antioxidants and immune-boosting ingredients.

day 9

Depending on your previous diet, you may have noticed that the variety of foods you eat has dramatically increased. Really focus on how new foods taste, smell and feel today and over the next few days – this will help you keep up the variety once you have finished the plan.

breakfast

wake-up smoothie
(see page 54)

2 slices of toast
Choose granary, barley or soya bread and top each with 1 teaspoon of peanut butter

snack

asparagus guacamole
Blend 75 g (3 oz) of cooked asparagus spears with 1 tablespoon of low-fat crème fraîche, and stir in a little chopped red onion, tomato and a squeeze of lemon juice. Serve with 2 carrots cut into crudités

lunch

cherry tomato and pasta salad
(see page 54), served with a salad of rocket and celery

snack

pot of low-fat fruit yogurt
150 g (5 oz)

did you know?

Not getting enough sleep makes cells more insulin resistant and may therefore promote fat storage. On top of this, fatigue is one of the main reasons we reach for sugary snacks and high-fat foods. Try to get 8 hours sleep a night.

dinner

quinoa with roasted vegetables
Cook 75 g (3 oz) quinoa according to the packet instructions. Serve with roasted vegetables, such as aubergines, mushrooms or peppers, and sprinkle with 25 g (1 oz) roasted almonds

ALTERNATIVE:
ready-made vegetarian lasagne
Choose one with less than 400 kcal (1680 kj) and serve with salad, as above

day 10

Have you noticed that your skin is looking better? The protein content of your diet is likely to have increased, so your skin, hair and nails will be growing stronger and healthier.

breakfast

Pumpkin Seed and Apricot Muesli (see recipe, page 45)

1 piece of fruit

snack

2 kiwi fruit or 2 handfuls of cherries

lunch

omelette made from 1 egg and 3 egg whites, filled with mushrooms and asparagus, served with 100 g (3½ oz) canned baked beans

snack

protein shake (see page 42), served with 100 g (3½ oz) of canned pears in natural juice

dinner

Spicy Lentil and Tomato Soup (see recipe, page 57), served with a 100 g (3½ oz) chunk of granary, barley or soya bread and a large green salad

did you know?

Chewing food properly increases the nutrients we absorb from it and also triggers the production of serotonin in the brain, which reduces appetite.

day 11

Don't waver now – you should really be able to notice your clothes feeling looser, particularly around your tummy. If you've been exercising as part of the plan, your thighs, bottom and calves should be looking and feeling firmer too.

breakfast

protein shake
(see page 42)

fruit plate
made from 1 sliced banana, 1 sliced pear, ½ mango and a handful of berries or cherries

ALTERNATIVE:
pot of low-fat yogurt
150 g (5 oz), served with a fruit plate, as above

snack

toast and avocado
2 slices of granary, soya or barley toast topped with ½ avocado, mashed

lunch

salad and crispbreads
Mixed-leaf salad (rocket, baby spinach, radicchio) topped with 6 cherry tomatoes, 5 black olives, 25 g (1 oz) of pine nuts, 1 teaspoon of olive oil and a squeeze of lemon juice. Serve with 3 rye crispbreads, each topped with 1 teaspoon of hummus

snack

cheese and grapes
25 g (1 oz) low-fat Edam cheese and 100 g (3½ oz) white grapes

dinner

Thai Noodles with Vegetables and Tofu
(see recipe, right)

ALTERNATIVE:
stir-fried tofu
Stir-fry 50 g (2 oz) of tofu per person with a selection of vegetables, a little soy sauce and a pinch of garlic. Serve with 25 g (1 oz) of dried egg noodles per person, cooked according to packet instructions

motivation tip

Are the kids' sweets tempting you every time you open the fridge? Put them in a covered part of the fridge so that you can't see them. Research shows that we eat twice as much food if it's in a visible place than if it's out of sight.

thai noodles with vegetables and tofu

preparation time: 20 minutes, plus marinating

cooking time: 40 minutes

serves 4

250 g (8 oz) tofu, diced

2 tablespoons dark soy sauce

1 teaspoon grated lime rind

1.8 litres (3 pints) vegetable stock

2 slices of fresh root ginger

2 garlic cloves

2 coriander sprigs

2 lemon grass stalks, crushed

1 red chilli, bruised

175 g (6 oz) dried egg noodles

125 g (4 oz) button mushrooms, sliced

2 large carrots, cut into matchsticks

125 g (4 oz) sugar snap peas

125 g (4 oz) Chinese cabbage, shredded

2 tablespoons chopped fresh coriander

1 Put the tofu in a shallow dish with the soy sauce and lime rind. Marinate for 30 minutes.

2 Meanwhile, put the vegetable stock into a large saucepan and add the ginger, garlic, coriander sprigs, lemon grass and chilli. Bring to the boil, reduce the heat, cover and simmer for 30 minutes.

3 Strain the vegetable stock into another saucepan, return to the boil and plunge in the noodles. Add the sliced mushrooms and marinated tofu with any remaining marinade. Reduce the heat and simmer gently for 4 minutes.

4 Stir in the carrots, sugar snap peas, Chinese cabbage and chopped coriander, cook for a further 3–4 minutes and serve.

kcal: **276 (1160 kj)**
protein: **18 g**
carbohydrate: **33 g**
fat: **6 g**
GI: **M**

nutrition tip:
Ginger is a metabolism-boosting spice. If you enjoy the taste, try a little shredded ginger on salads, or a ginger tea to power up your diet further.

day 12

By now the concentration of very low-GI foods in your diet should have ensured that your insulin levels are well controlled – time therefore to introduce a treat or two.

breakfast

Walnut and Banana Sunrise Smoothie
(see recipe, page 63)

bowl of cereal
25 g (1 oz) noodle-shaped bran cereal, topped with 150 ml (¼ pint) of skimmed milk and 50 g (2 oz) of berries

snack

small tub of tzatziki
125 g (4 oz), served with 2 carrots cut into crudités

lunch

sandwich
2 slices of granary, barley or soya bread spread with a little mustard and filled with 1 sliced hard-boiled egg or 25 g (1 oz) of cream cheese, and sliced tomatoes, cucumber and lettuce

bean salad
(see page 50), 100 g (3½ oz)

snack

sweet treat
choose from: a 30 g (1 oz) bar of plain or milk chocolate, 2 scoops of any low-fat ice cream or frozen yogurt, or 2 chocolate biscuits

dinner

burger and chips
1 vegetarian burger served with 100 g (3½ oz) of chipped sweet potatoes and 75 g (3 oz) of peas

did you know?

The taste of sugary foods may come as a shock after so long without them. Your taste buds will have become used to your new diet, so you may even find that you no longer like the taste of high sugar snacks!

day 13

One more day to go, so really focus on your efforts today. Walk everywhere you can, make the most of any down time to do some vigorous exercise and make sure you drink those fluid-busting 8 glasses of water. The bigger the result on the scales tomorrow the better you'll feel.

breakfast

Buckwheat Pancakes
(see recipe, page 51), served with 1 sliced banana and 1 teaspoon of maple syrup

glass of soya or skimmed milk
150 ml (¼ pint)

ALTERNATIVE:
2 slices of fruit bread
topped with 25 g (1 oz) ricotta or cream cheese, and 100 g (3½ oz) mixed berries

snack

1 pear

lunch

caesar salad
made from unlimited iceberg lettuce, mixed with 1 tablespoon low-fat vegetarian caesar salad dressing and 1 oz (25 g) of grated Parmesan. Top with 75 g (3 oz) of antipasto, such as roasted aubergine, mushroom or peppers (drain the oil and place on a piece of kitchen towel before adding to the salad)

snack

strawberries and cream
100 g (3½ oz) of strawberries topped with 1 teaspoon of whipped cream or yogurt

dinner

Vegetable Curry
(see recipe, page 67), served with 25 g (1 oz) of dried basmati rice and 50 g (2 oz) of dried lentils, cooked according to packet instructions, plus a serving of spinach sprinkled with a little lemon juice and nutmeg

ALTERNATIVE:
ready-made vegetable curry
Choose one with under 300 kcal (1260 kj). Serve with rice, lentils and spinach, as above

motivational tip

When you exercise, your metabolic rate stays a little higher than normal for up to 12 hours, depending on the intensity of the exercise.

day 14

You are at the end of your official diet – but this doesn't mean you have to give up slimming. You can either repeat the two-week plan until you've lost all the weight you want to lose – or use the GI rules and the calorie charts to devise your own regime.

breakfast

cheese on toast
2 slices of granary, soya or barley bread, each topped with 25 g (1 oz) of grated cheese, and grilled. Serve with grilled tomatoes and grilled mushrooms

glass of unsweetened orange juice
150 ml (¼ pint)

snack

1 banana

lunch

falafel salad
6 grilled falafel balls, served with a large salad of rocket, bean sprouts, tomato, green pepper and ½ avocado

snack

½ mango
topped with 75 g (3 oz) of low-fat cottage cheese

dinner

Braised Lentils with Mushrooms and Gremolata
(see recipe, right), served with 50 g (2 oz) of steamed broccoli

ALTERNATIVE:
grilled mushrooms and quick lentil salad
2 grilled portobello mushrooms, served with 200 g (7 oz) of quick lentil salad (see page 46), and a large salad of rocket, cucumber, and 3 sun-dried tomatoes

motivation **booster**

Congratulations! Sticking to a diet plan for more than a few days is something most people find incredibly hard to do. Now that you've managed two weeks your new eating patterns will have started to become a habit, so carrying on with the plan will be relatively easy.

braised lentils with mushrooms and gremolata

preparation time: 15 minutes

cooking time: 30 minutes

serves 2

2 tablespoons olive oil

1 onion, chopped

1 celery stick, sliced

1 carrot, sliced

75 g (3 oz) Puy lentils, rinsed

300 ml (½ pint) vegetable stock

125 ml (4 fl oz) dry white wine

1 bay leaf

1 tablespoon chopped thyme

175 g (6 oz) mushrooms, sliced

salt and pepper

GREMOLATA

1 tablespoon chopped parsley

finely grated rind of ½ lemon

1 garlic clove, chopped

1 Heat 1 tablespoon of the olive oil in a saucepan and fry the onion, celery and carrots for 3 minutes. Add the lentils, stock, wine, herbs, a generous sprinkling of pepper and a small pinch of salt. Bring to the boil, reduce the heat and simmer gently, uncovered, for about 20 minutes or until the lentils are tender.

2 Meanwhile, mix together the ingredients for the gremolata.

3 Heat the remaining oil in a frying pan, add the mushrooms and fry quickly for about 2 minutes until golden.

4 Ladle the lentils on to serving plates, top with the mushrooms and serve scattered with the gremolata.

kcal: **326 (1370 kj)**
protein: **12 g**
carbohydrate: **24 g**
fat: **17 g**
GI: **L**

nutrition tip:
Lentils are a great source of protein and iron, and make a filling base for any dish – or a great side dish served on their own.

GI **indulgences**

If you need to increase the calories you are eating on the weight-loss programme, or just want a low-calorie, low-GI snack between meals – here are 50 suggestions to try.

Around **50 kcal (210 kj)**

- 1 apple, orange, pear or other medium fruit
- 175 g (6 oz) small fruits, such as berries or cherries
- 3 satsumas, kiwis or apricots
- 150 g (5 oz) very low-fat fruit yogurt
- 3 tablespoons of salsa with 3 celery sticks for dipping
- 1 oatcake topped with 1 teaspoon of low-sugar jam
- 15 olives
- 200 ml (7 fl oz) of carrot juice
- 150 ml (5 fl oz) of skimmed milk or 100 ml (3½ fl oz) of soya milk
- 5 almonds

- vegetable plate with 200 g (8 oz) of celery, carrots, cucumber and cherry tomatoes
- 75 g (3 oz) of strawberries with 1 teaspoon of reduced-fat cream
- 2 slices of lean ham, one tomato and a little mustard
- prawn cocktail of 50 g (2 oz) of prawns in ½ teaspoon of low-fat cocktail sauce, served on iceberg lettuce
- 1 rye crispbread topped with 1 low-fat cheese triangle
- 25 g (1 oz) of dried apricots

Around 150 kcal (630 kj)

- 1 slice of granary, soya or barley bread with a mashed banana
- 1 wholemeal tortilla wrap spread with mustard and filled with 25 g (1 oz) of lean ham and one tomato
- 2 rye crispbreads spread with 50 g (2 oz) of low-fat cream cheese topped with 25 g (1 oz) of berries or 1 teaspoon of low-sugar jam
- 1 slice of toast topped with 3 oz (75 g) of canned baked beans
- 50 g (2 oz) of vegetarian pâté with crudités made from 2 carrots
- ½ avocado filled with 2 tablespoons of salsa or 25 g (1 oz) of prawns
- 25 g (1 oz) of noodle-shaped bran cereal topped with 150 ml (¼ pint) of skimmed milk and 25 g (1 oz) of berries
- 40 g (1½ oz) low-fat Edam cheese and 50 g (2 oz) of grapes
- 4 chicken nuggets

- 25 peanuts, cashews or pistachios
- 10 olives and 6 salted almonds
- 25 g (1 oz) of plain, white or milk chocolate
- 25 g (1 oz) of chocolate-covered peanuts
- smoothie made from 200 ml (7 fl oz) of soya milk, ½ banana and 50 g (2 oz) strawberries
- 1 slice of thin-crust vegetarian pizza
- 1 boiled egg and 2 rye crispbreads spread with 1 teaspoon of yeast extract
- 4 falafel balls with 2 teaspoons of tzatziki
- 25 g (1 oz) of Parma ham with 100 g (3½ oz) cantaloupe melon

Around 100 kcal (420 kj)

- ½ apple topped with 1 teaspoon of peanut butter
- ½ pear topped with 1 teaspoon of chocolate spread
- 2 rye crispbreads topped with 25 g (1 oz) of low-fat hummus or 75 g (3 oz) of tzatziki
- 1 slice of granary, soya or barley bread topped with 25 g (1 oz) of tuna in spring water, or cottage cheese with pineapple
- 75 g (3 oz) of shredded chicken or crabsticks mixed with 1 teaspoon of salad cream and ½ sliced green pepper
- 1 protein shake (see page 42)
- ½ mango topped with 50 g (2 oz) of cottage cheese
- 300 g (10 oz) can of slimmer's tomato or vegetable soup
- 1 slice of fruit bread, toasted, topped with ½ teaspoon of low-fat spread
- 25 g (1 oz) of plain sponge cake
- 50 g (2 oz) of low-fat vanilla ice cream
- 50 g (2 oz) of low-fat hummus or 175 g (6 oz) of tzatziki with crudités made from 3 oz (75 g) of cucumber
- 5 Brazil nuts
- 4 celery sticks spread with 2 oz (50 g) of low-fat cream cheese
- 1 tablespoon of sunflower or pumpkin seeds
- 50 g (2 oz) fromage frais with 2 teaspoons of muesli stirred in

GI GALVANIZER PLAN

This low-GI plan will guarantee you have optimum energy when you most need it.

Most of us feel we need more energy – part of the problem is that we have just got too busy for our own good. However, there is also the fact that the high-GI diets that most of us eat actually sap energy, not provide it. By following the GI Galvanizer Plan and focusing on low-GI foods and adhering to the rules on page 37 you can dramatically boost your energy levels and banish feelings of fatigue, enabling you to live your life to the full.

day 1

Time to get started. Just follow each meal as directed, but try to give the daily energizing tips a try too. They will help power up the plan.

breakfast

bowl of porridge
made from rolled oats and skimmed or soya milk. Top with a handful of blueberries

glass of orange juice

snack

small handful of almonds, peanuts or cashews

energizing tip

Stimulating blood flow to your brain is an instant energizer. To do this, use your fingertips to rub quickly all over your scalp as if you were washing your hair.

lunch

grilled chicken sandwich
on granary, barley or soya bread, or two slices of toasted bread with hummus

salad
of asparagus, cherry tomatoes, and yellow peppers on a bed of alfalfa sprouts

snack

3 satsumas

1 banana

dinner

Braised Lentils with Mushrooms and Gremolata
(see recipe, page 89), served with spinach and broccoli

energy **provider**

Asparagus and alfalfa
Both neutralize the natural toxin ammonia, which is produced within our bodies and makes us sleepy.

day 2

Energy can be as much a state of mind as a physical thing. Today, spend 5 minutes thinking about all the good things your new diet will bring. The positive feelings should maximize results.

breakfast

bowl of cereal
Choose noodle-shaped bran cereal, topped with skimmed or soya milk and a chopped banana

glass of fruit juice

snack

toast with peanut butter
Choose granary, soya or barley bread

lunch

Moroccan Tomato and Chickpea Salad
(see recipe, page 41), served with grilled king prawns or feta cheese

snack

1 apple

1 kiwi fruit

dinner

spaghetti
topped with carbonara or cheese sauce. Serve with a large green salad containing alfalfa sprouts and spinach leaves

energy **provider**

Breakfast cereals
Not only filled with fibre, these are normally fortified with iron and B vitamins.

energizing tip

Focus on your breathing: oxygen dramatically energizes our systems. Try to breathe deeply throughout the day, expanding your lungs on the inhale, compressing your abdomen on the exhale to really flush out that old air.

day 3

Exercise dramatically boosts energy – from today try to build 30 minutes of activity into your day as well as following the plan.

breakfast

French toast
made with slices of granary, soya or barley bread soaked in a little egg and fried in a pan moistened with an oil spray (see page 47). Serve with strawberries and apple chunks

snack

1 orange

1 banana

lunch

carton of bean or lentil soup
served with a large green salad

cheese on toast
2 slices of granary, barley or soya bread topped with a little low-fat cheese, and grilled

snack

pot of low-fat yogurt
sprinkled with a little muesli

dinner

Salmon Fishcakes
(see recipe, right), served with Tomato and Pepper Salsa (see recipe, page 41). Serve with asparagus spears

ALTERNATIVE:
Quorn™ steaks or vegetarian burgers
served with Tomato and Pepper Salsa (see recipe, page 41) and pasta spirals

energy **provider**

Water
The first sign of dehydration is fatigue. Fluid-heavy foods like celery, cucumber, fennel, apples, pears, grapefruit and grapes also energize.

energizing tip

Work with your natural energy levels. The time you are most alert is set at birth – some of us are morning people, others are more awake later in the day. By focusing on harder tasks when your natural energy is strongest, you will feel more dynamic – and get more done.

salmon fishcakes

preparation time: 20 minutes

cooking time: 30 minutes

serves 6

500 g (1 lb) new potatoes, chopped

grated rind and juice of 1 lemon

4 tablespoons milk

1 bunch of spring onions, sliced

½ teaspoon cayenne pepper

2 x 200 g (7 oz) cans salmon in water or brine, drained and flaked

2 tablespoons plain flour

1 egg, beaten

100 g (3½ oz) fresh white breadcrumbs

1 tablespoon olive oil

salt and pepper

1 Cook the potatoes in a pan of lightly salted boiling water until tender. Mash and stir in the lemon rind and juice, milk, spring onions, cayenne pepper and the salmon. Season to taste with salt and pepper.

2 Form the mixture into 8 patties. Dip them in flour, then the egg, then the breadcrumbs and place on a lightly oiled baking sheet

3 Drizzle over the remaining oil and cook in a preheated oven at 200°C (400°F), Gas Mark 6, for 12–15 minutes, turning once, until golden and piping hot.

kcal: **385 (1617 kj)**
protein: **25 g**
carbohydrate: **46 g**
fat: **12 g**
GI: **M**

nutrition tip:
As well as providing energy, the essential fatty acids found in fish like salmon, mackerel, bass and herring help protect the heart and arteries from damage.

day 4

By now you should have noticed a significant change in your energy levels: after-lunch slumps should be a thing of the past and you should be sleeping better, making mornings a brighter time of day.

breakfast

Pumpkin Seed and Apricot Muesli (see recipe, page 45) or a bowl of low-sugar muesli. Top with skimmed or soya milk

½ grapefruit

snack

canned pears or peaches in natural juice

energizing tip

Try to get some sunlight, or at least natural light, every day. Sunlight helps switch off the production of melatonin, the hormone that makes us feel sleepy.

lunch

stuffed tortilla and salad
1 wholemeal tortilla wrap stuffed with tuna fish or ½ avocado, sliced, alfalfa sprouts and tomato. Serve with a salad of lettuce, cucumber, celery, chopped apple and walnuts mixed with 1 tablespoon of low-fat mayonnaise

snack

protein shake
(see page 42), and a handful of berries

ALTERNATIVE:
smoothie
made from soya milk, soya yogurt and a handful of berries

dinner

Melanzane Parmigiana (see recipe, right), served with couscous and dark green cabbage or kale

energy **provider**

Watercress
This contains high levels of chlorophyll that boosts oxygen in our system. Also try wheatgrass, dark green lettuce and dark green cabbage.

melanzane parmigiana

preparation time: 10 minutes

cooking time: 50 minutes

serves 6

6 aubergines

2 tablespoons extra virgin olive oil

2 x 400 g (13 oz) cans chopped tomatoes

2 garlic cloves, crushed

250 g (8 oz) Cheddar cheese, grated

50 g (2 oz) Parmesan cheese, grated

1 Trim the aubergines and cut lengthways into thick slices. Brush them with half the oil and place on 2 large baking sheets. Roast at the top of a preheated oven at 200°C (400°F), Gas Mark 6, for 10 minutes on each side until golden and tender.

2 Meanwhile, place the tomatoes and garlic in a saucepan and bring to the boil. Reduce the heat and simmer for 10 minutes, then season with salt and pepper.

3 Spoon a little of the tomato into an ovenproof dish and top with a layer of aubergines and some of the Cheddar. Continue with the layers, finishing with a layer of Cheddar on top. Sprinkle over the Parmesan and bake for 30 minutes until the cheese is bubbling and golden.

kcal: **262 (1100 kj)**
protein: **18 g**
carbohydrate: **8 g**
fat: **18 g**
GI: **L**

nutrition tip:
Cheese can also be an energizing food as it contains the amino acid tyrosine which helps manufacture the alertness chemicals norepinephidrine and dopamine.

day 5

If you started this plan on a Monday it will now be Friday. Make the most of your new-found energy and go out and have fun tonight.

breakfast

fruit plate
1 orange, a handful of blueberries, ½ mango and a handful of grapes

2 oatcakes
spread with a little ricotta or cream cheese

snack

glass of skimmed or soya milk

handful of sunflower or pumpkin seeds

lunch

antipasto plate
choose a selection of vegetable antipasto and serve with grilled chicken breast, fresh mussels or reduced-fat mozzarella cheese

snack

asparagus guacamole
(see page 82), served with 2 carrots cut into crudités

dinner

Vegetable Curry
(see recipe, page 67), served with basmati rice, spinach sprinkled with nutmeg and lentils

energizing tip

Aromatherapy oils are a potent way to rebalance energy levels. Try using them in the bath or, for an instant pick-up, place 2–3 drops on a tissue and breathe in the scent deeply. The best energizers are grapefruit, peppermint and rosemary oils. Don't try this while pregnant.

energy **provider**

Blueberries
Vitamin C is an energizing nutrient and blueberries are packed with it (as are oranges, grapefruit, red peppers, green peppers and kiwi fruit).

day 6

The careful balance of carbohydrates and protein on the GI Galvanizer plan don't just keep you energized throughout the day – they also ensure that night time is more restful. By now you should be sleeping better, so make the most of your brighter mornings and get out and enjoy the day!

breakfast

Buckwheat Pancakes
(see recipe, page 51), topped with blueberries and crème fraîche

snack

1 orange

lunch

roast beef
(fat removed), served with mashed or roasted sweet potatoes, cabbage, carrots and peas and a little gravy

ALTERNATIVE:
cauliflower cheese
served with vegetables, as above

snack

handful of dried apricots

dinner

Bean Salad
(see recipe, page 51), served with canned salmon, grilled chicken or low-fat cheese. Add some sliced beetroot (remembering it's a high-GI food so keep portions small), sliced yellow peppers and grated carrot

energy **provider**

Red meat
Iron deficiency causes lowered oxygen levels and tiredness. If you don't eat meat, dark green leafy vegetables and dried fruits are also good sources of iron.

energizing tip

Tackle a worry: the average person spends 27 hours worrying each week, leading to stress and low energy. Try to deal with one thing that is nagging at you today and feel the weight around your shoulders lift.

day 7

This is the end of your formal energizing plan – but hopefully it has shown you the positive benefits that focusing on energy-giving, low-GI foods can bring. To carry on, just make up your own menus using the rules on page 35 and the charts on page 118.

breakfast

poached egg
served with canned baked beans and grilled mushrooms

½ grapefruit

snack

4 celery sticks
spread with peanut butter or cream cheese

lunch

stir-fried vegetables
Try bok choy, carrot, mushrooms, asparagus and mangetout, stir-fried with prawns or tofu, soy sauce and garlic

snack

pot of low-fat fruit yogurt

pear or apple

dinner

Chicken or Bean Enchiladas
(see recipe, right), served with a large salad of lettuce, cherry tomatoes and celery

energizing tip

A good night's sleep is vital for energy. According to Ayurvedic medicine, between 10pm and 6am, when the body is in restorative mode, is the best time to get it. If you find it hard to drop off, include lettuce in your evening meal: it contains lactucarium, a natural sedative.

energy provider

Spicy foods are energizers as the feel of chillies and other hot spices on the tongue triggers the production of endorphins, energy-boosting and mood-enhancing chemicals in the brain.

chicken enchiladas

To make **Bean Enchiladas,** omit the chicken and double the quantity of beans.

preparation time: 15 minutes

cooking time: 30 minutes

serves 6

2 teaspoons vegetable oil

1 large onion, chopped

250 g (8 oz) canned pinto beans, rinsed and drained

300 g (10 oz) cooked chicken breast, skinned and cubed

4 green chillies, deseeded and chopped

1 teaspoon dried oregano

1 large tomato, chopped

½ teaspoon chilli powder

½ teaspoon ground cumin

400 g (13 oz) can tomatoes

12 wholemeal tortillas

6 tablespoons pre-prepared salsa

75 g (3 oz) low-fat mozzarella, grated

1 Heat the oil in a saucepan, add the onion and cook for about 5 minutes until softened. Stir in the beans, chicken (if using), chillies, oregano and fresh tomato. Warm through, then remove the pan from the heat.

energy provider

Beans and pulses
These provide energizing B vitamins and iron.

2 Blend the tomatoes in a food processor or blender. Place the chilli powder, cumin and blended tomatoes in a saucepan and simmer for 2 minutes. Remove from the heat.

3 Dip each tortilla into the blended tomato mixture and set aside on a plate. Fill each one with 3 tablespoons of the chicken mixture. Roll up and place, seam side down, in an ovenproof dish. Spoon the salsa over the enchiladas, sprinkle with the cheese and bake in a preheated oven at 180°C (350°F), Gas Mark 4 for about 20 minutes.

kcal: **380 (1596 kj)**
protein: **24 g**
carbohydrate: **50 g**
fat: **9 g**
GI: **L**

GI FOR LIFE PLAN

This maintenance plan will help you to keep the weight off, stay healthy and protect against illness.

This plan aims to maximize the benefits of eating low-GI foods by focusing your daily diet on foods with known anti-ageing effects. This means lots of fruit and vegetables, plenty of beans, pulses and whole grains – but also antioxidant-filled foods like chocolate and red wine. By following the GI for Life Plan, you are increasing your chances of a long and healthy life.

day 1

The thing you'll really notice today is just how easy eating for a longer life is. With 'sinful' treat foods like sour cream and steak it may seem that you aren't eating healthily – but you are.

breakfast

bowl of muesli
topped with a little skimmed or soya milk. Add a banana and a handful of strawberries or raspberries

cup of tea
(aim for another 3 today)

snack

broccoli florets
dipped in low-fat soured cream mixed with some chives

lunch

sandwich
Choose granary, soya or barley bread, and fill with canned salmon or a boiled egg, and a handful of watercress

tomato soup

snack

2 pieces of fruit

pot of low-fat yogurt

dinner

lean sirloin steak
(remove all obvious fat), served with lentils and a large salad of rocket, avocado and celery

glass of red wine

ALTERNATIVE:
Chickpea and Chard Tortilla
(see recipe, right), served with salad and wine, as above

live longer tip

Be more active. People who burn 1500 calories a week on gentle activities such as gardening, golf or walking, live 1.6 years longer than people with less active lifestyles.

chickpea and chard tortilla

preparation time: 20 minutes

cooking time: 15 minutes

serves 4

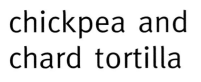

4 tablespoons olive oil

1 onion, chopped

1 red pepper, cored, deseeded and chopped

4 garlic cloves

½ teaspoon dried chilli flakes

500 g (1 lb) chard or spinach leaves

400 g (13 oz) can chickpeas, rinsed and drained

6 eggs

2 tablespoons chopped parsley

salt and pepper

1 Heat half the oil in a large, nonstick frying pan. Add the onion, red pepper, garlic and chilli flakes, and fry gently for 10 minutes until softened and lightly golden.

2 Meanwhile, wash and dry the chard and cut away the thick central stems. Shred the leaves. Stir the chard into the onion mixture together with the chickpeas and cook gently for 5 minutes.

top 3 age-fighters

banana A high-potassium food which helps lower blood pressure

tea Packed with heart-protective antioxidants

broccoli One of the cancer-fighting cruciferous vegetables – even just half a cup a week helps your health

3 Beat the eggs in a bowl with the parsley and a little salt and pepper. Stir in the chickpea mixture. Wipe out the pan and add the remaining oil. Pour in the egg mixture and cook over a low heat for 10 minutes, until the tortilla is almost cooked through.

4 Carefully slide the tortilla out onto a large plate, invert the pan over the plate, then flip the tortilla back into the pan up the other way. Continue to cook for a further 5 minutes until cooked through. Serve cut into wedges.

kcal: **426 (1790 kj)**
protein: **23 g**
carbohydrate: **20 g**
fat: **29 g**
GI: **L**

day 2

In a diet for life it is important that meals are quick and easy to prepare. You'll really see the benefits of this today, with 3 superfast, delicious meals to try.

breakfast

scrambled eggs
made from 2 eggs and a little butter and milk. Serve with smoked salmon on 1 slice of granary, soya or barley toast

glass of fruit juice

snack

1 apple and 1 pear

lunch

crudités plate
made from celery, carrots, cherry tomatoes and mangetout

small tub of hummus

snack

smoothie
made from skimmed or soya milk, 1 banana, a handful of blueberries and a handful of strawberries

dinner

Thai-style Fish and Mushroom Kebabs
(see recipe, right), served with couscous and spinach

ALTERNATIVE:
Thai-style Tofu and Mushroom Kebabs
(see recipe, right), replacing the fish with firm tofu. Serve with couscous and spinach

top 3 **age-fighters**

• **fish** Both oily fish and white fish protect against the effects of age, cutting the risk of stroke, heart attack and arthritis

• **blueberries** Part of the potent purple foods family that contain the highest number of antioxidants

• **spinach** High in a compound called lutein that fights heart disease and age-related blindness

thai-style fish and mushroom kebabs

preparation time: 15 minutes, plus marinating

cooking time: 10 minutes

serves 4

500–750 g (1–1½ lb) firm white fish (monkfish, swordfish, cod or haddock)

1 courgette, cut into 8 pieces

1 onion, quartered and layers separated

8 mushrooms

vegetable oil, for brushing

MARINADE

grated rind and juice of 2 limes

1 garlic clove, finely chopped

2 tablespoons finely sliced fresh root ginger

2 chillies, deseeded and finely chopped

2 lemon grass stalks, finely chopped

handful of finely chopped coriander

1 glass of red wine

2 tablespoons sesame oil

pepper

live longer tip

Floss your teeth. Strange but true, flossing reduces the risk of heart disease as the bacteria that cause gum disease also contribute to furring of the arteries.

1 Combine the marinade ingredients in a large bowl. Cut the fish into large cubes and add to the marinade with the courgettes, onion and mushrooms. Cover and refrigerate for 1 hour.

2 Brush the rack of a grill pan lightly with oil to prevent the kebabs from sticking. Thread 4 skewers alternately with the chunks of fish, mushrooms, courgette and onion. Brush with a little oil and grill under a preheated hot grill for about 10 minutes, turning regularly.

kcal: **195 (819 kJ)**
protein: **30 g**
carbohydrate: **3 g**
fat: **5 g**
GI: **L**

day 3

As well as protecting your future, don't forget this plan also provides the day-to-day health boosts of eating low GI – more energy and better moods. These should be starting about now.

breakfast

bowl of porridge
made from rolled oats with water or a little skimmed or soya milk. Top with some sultanas and half an apple, chopped

snack

2 rye crispbreads
topped with thin slices of low-fat Cheddar cheese

lunch

smoked mackerel on toast
Smoked mackerel or sardines on 2 slices of granary, soya or barley toast. Top with rocket or sliced tomato

fruit salad
made from any four different fruits, chopped and sprinkled with orange juice. Strawberries, kiwi fruit, satsumas and banana work well together

ALTERNATIVE:

1 poached egg on a bed of spinach
served with a slice of granary toast, and fruit salad as above

snack

handful of walnuts or brazil nuts

dinner

Thai Noodles with Vegetables and Tofu
(see recipe, page 85)

top 3 age-fighters

• **oats** Calcium helps protect bones as we age – and oats contain high levels. They also lower cholesterol

• **nuts** People who eat these more than 5 times a week live 10 years longer than those who don't. Heart-protective vitamin E and the antioxidant selenium are thought to be the reason

• **tofu** High in cancer-preventive phytoestrogens, all soya products also help detox the body

live longer tip

Think happy thoughts. Optimists live 10 years longer than pessimists, say researchers at the University of Kentucky.

day 4

Research has shown that people who eat the largest variety of foods tend to live longer than those who eat an unvaried diet. Today you'll be eating over twenty different foods – a recipe for a long and healthy life.

breakfast

bowl of bran cereal
Choose noodle-shaped bran cereal, topped with soya or skimmed milk and 2 handfuls of berries

½ grapefruit

snack

handful of apricots

lunch

½ avocado
topped with prawns or walnuts tossed in a little cocktail dressing or mayonnaise. Serve with a large salad of red cabbage, carrot and onion

snack

celery sticks or pear slices
dipped in peanut butter or cream cheese

dinner

Warm Aubergine Salad
(see recipe, page 53), served with grilled salmon steaks or slices of buffalo mozzarella. Add 1–2 slices of granary, soya or barley bread

glass of red wine

live longer tip

Lose weight – it has been calculated that every 0.5 kg (1 lb) you are overweight, knocks 36 days off your life, so keep to a healthy weight. The newest way to check this is to measure the circumference of your neck: if it is less than 37 cm (14½ inches) for a man or 34 cm (13½ inches) for a woman, you are not overweight, according to Israeli doctors.

top 3 age-fighters

• **avocado** High in the antioxidant glutathione, high levels of which are linked to longevity

• **olive oil** Contains heart-protecting vitamin E – no surprise that people live longer in countries with the highest olive oil use

• **wine** Like other purple fruits and vegetables, red grapes are high in antioxidants. Don't go over safe limits – these are 1–2 glasses a day for women and 2–3 glasses for men

day 5

You should notice by now that hunger pangs are a thing of the past. That's because your insulin levels are balancing out, preventing those appetite-stimulating energy crashes.

breakfast

breakfast platter
Sliced apple, cheese slices, celery, walnuts and cottage cheese, served with 3 rye crispbreads

glass of orange juice

snack

toast and peanut butter
2 slices of granary, soya or barley bread, toasted and topped with peanut butter

lunch

Sweet Potato and Coconut Soup
(see recipe, right), or a carton of ready-made bean-based soup, served with a large salad of green beans, chickpeas, chopped tomato, onion and 1 boiled egg

snack

4 squares of plain chocolate

glass of skimmed or soya milk

dinner

Griddled Chicken with Pearl Barley
(see recipe, page 65), served with a side salad of mixed salad leaves drizzled with balsamic vinegar

ALTERNATIVE:
Quorn™ Steak with Pearl Barley
(see recipe, page 65), replacing the chicken with a Quorn™ steak or some grilled vegetables. Serve with salad, as above

top 3 age-fighters

• **sweet potatoes** Packed with antioxidants, they are the ultimate anti-ageing food

• **garlic** Helps prevent arterial furring – eating garlic daily is said to turn back your heart age by 13 years

• **chocolate** Contains as many antioxidants as prunes, which cancels out its high fat content

sweet potato and coconut soup

preparation time: 25 minutes

cooking time: 50 minutes

serves 4

4 tablespoons olive oil

2 onions, finely chopped

500 g (1 lb) sweet potatoes, peeled and roughly chopped

2 garlic cloves, crushed

7.5 cm (3 inch) piece of fresh root ginger, peeled and finely chopped

½ teaspoon dried chilli flakes

600 ml (1 pint) water

400 ml (14 fl oz) can coconut milk

2 tablespoons grated coconut

salt and pepper

1 Heat the oil and gently fry the onion for about 10 minutes or until golden brown. Add the chopped sweet potatoes and fry for 4–5 minutes or until the flesh has begun to brown.

live longer tip

Take vitamin C. Women who take 300–400 mg of vitamin C a day get protection from heart disease that will make them live one year longer, say researchers at the University of California. Men, as they are at a greater risk of heart disease, get six years of life extension from the same dose.

2 Add the crushed garlic, chopped ginger, dried chilli, the measured water and the coconut milk. Now sprinkle in the grated coconut, salt and pepper and bring to a fast simmer (but do not boil). Cover the pan and simmer for 30–35 minutes.

3 When the sweet potato is tender, allow the soup to cool a little, then blend in batches in a food processor. Return to the pan, check the seasoning, heat through and serve.

kcal: **406 (1705 kj)**
protein: **4 g**
carbohydrate: **35 g**
fat: **8 g**
GI: **M**

day 6

While 5 portions of fruit and vegetables a day are recommended for good health, 10 servings are recommended for superhealth and illness prevention. If you think that sounds tricky, bear in mind that you've achieved that every day on this plan.

breakfast

Summer Fruits With Honeyed Oat Topping
(see recipe, right)

ALTERNATIVE:
bowl of porridge
made from rolled oats and water or skimmed milk. Top with chopped apricots and strawberries

snack

pot of low-fat fruit yogurt

lunch

Herby Lentil Salad with Bacon
(see recipe, page 47), served with a salad of baby spinach and cherry tomatoes

ALTERNATIVE:
Herby Lentil Salad with Feta Cheese
(see recipe, page 47), replacing the bacon with crumbled feta cheese

snack

vegetable juice
made from 5 carrots, 1 apple and 2 celery sticks

2 rye crispbreads
topped with peanut butter

dinner

grilled trout fillet or Portobello mushrooms
served with mashed yams or sweet potatoes, Brussels sprouts and peas

top 3 age-fighters

• **carrots** Powerful detoxifiers of the body, carrots are also high in the antioxidant betacarotene

• **lentils** Australian researchers comparing lifespans and diets found those with a diet high in beans and pulses lived longest

• **Brussels sprouts** These contain sulforaphane, an ingredient researchers say could be the most powerful cancer preventer in the world

summer fruits with honeyed oat topping

preparation time: 5 minutes

serves 1

4 apricots, pitted and halved

4 strawberries, hulled and halved

1 dessertspoon clear honey

1 tablespoon Greek yogurt

1 tablespoon medium rolled oats

1 tablespoon toasted almonds

1 Put the apricots and strawberries in a bowl. Add the Greek yogurt and honey and sprinkle the oats and almonds over the top.

kcal: **275 (1158 kj)**
protein: **9 g**
carbohydrate: **36 g**
fat: **12 g**
GI: **L**

live longer tip

Learn to handle stress. One thing the 100-year-olds in the New England Centenarian Study have in common is that they don't let stress get them down.

day 7

This is the last day of the official plan, but remember it's only the beginning of the rest of your life. Use the recipes throughout this book and what you've learned to keep eating the low GI way, harnessing all the health benefits it can bring.

breakfast

French toast
made with slices of granary, soya or barley bread soaked in a little egg and fried in a pan moistened with an oil spray (see page 47). Serve with canned baked beans

snack

handful of berries with yogurt

lunch

Tabbouleh Salad
(see recipe, page 49), served with grilled red and yellow peppers and a scoop of hummus

snack

fruit salad
made with any 4 pieces of fruit sprinkled with orange or apple juice

dinner

Pasta with Tomato, Spinach and Ricotta
(see recipe, right), served with mangetout

top 3 **age-fighters**

• **baked beans** These have the same benefits as other beans and pulses, but their convenience means they deserve a special mention

• **peppers** Packed with vitamin C, peppers are also a great representative of the red, yellow and orange foods family, members of which contain vital antioxidants called carotenoids

• **tomato sauce** Packed with the cancer-fighting nutrient lycopene

pasta with tomato, spinach and ricotta

preparation time: 10 minutes

cooking time: 10–15 minutes

serves 4

375 g (12 oz) dried pasta shapes, such as penne

1 teaspoon olive oil

1 garlic clove, crushed

1 onion, sliced

½ teaspoon dried chilli flakes

700 g (1 lb 7 oz) jar passata

250 g (8 oz) baby spinach

150 g (5 oz) ricotta cheese

1 Cook the pasta in lightly salted boiling water for 12 minutes, or according to packet instructions, and drain well.

2 Meanwhile, heat the oil in a saucepan, add the garlic and onion and fry for 3–4 minutes. Add the chilli flakes and continue to fry for 1 minute.

live longer tip

Quit smoking. It is the best thing you can do to help your health – and maximize your chance of living longer.

3 Stir in the passata and simmer for 2 minutes. Add the spinach and ricotta, stir until the spinach has wilted, then simmer for 3–4 minutes. Toss the pasta through the sauce, season to taste with salt and pepper and serve.

kcal: **432 (1814 kj)**
protein: **18 g**
carbohydrate: **79 g**
fat: **7 g**
GI: **L**

GI CHARTS

This is the section for those who need to adapt the calorie count for their diet. Here you will find calorie counts for every food included in the GI weight-loss diets.

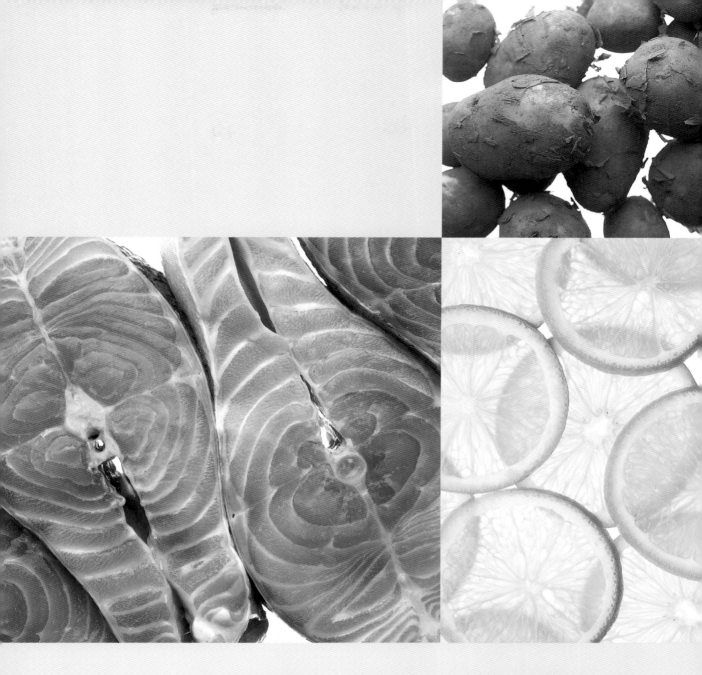

However, this is also the section for anyone who wants to take low-GI eating into their daily life. Listed here is the GI rating for over 300 day-to-day foods – everything from alfalfa sprouts to yogurt. Using these charts, you can make GI eating the permanent way to good health, increased energy, a slimmer figure – and possibly even a longer life.

Using the **charts**

Foods are listed in alphabetical order, as well as under section headings, such as Beans and pulses, to make comparisons easy. In the first column, the foods are marked clearly as high, medium, or low GI. The next column tells you how many calories (kcal) or kilojoules (kj) there are in 25 g (1 oz) of the food (or 100 ml (3½ fl oz) if it's a liquid).

* Items marked with an asterisk are pure protein foods that have such a negligible effect on blood sugar that, while not officially measured, their glycaemic index is assumed to be low. Please note that processing (for example, beefburgers rather than beef steak), adding breadcrumbs, butter or sauces, could change the GI of these foods, so all measurements (unless a processed product is noted) are for the pure product, such as a fresh chicken breast or fresh fish fillet.

A

Alfalfa	(l)	7 kcal (29 kj)
Almonds	(l)	172 kcal (722 kj)
Anchovies	(l)*	76 kcal (320 kj)
Apple	(l)	13 kcal (55 kj)
Apple juice	(l)	43 kcal (180 kj)
Apricots	(m)	8 kcal (34 kj)
Apricots (canned)	(m)	18 kcal (76 kj)
Apricots (dried)	(l)	53 kcal (223 kj)
Artichoke	(l)	13 kcal (55 kj)
Asparagus	(l)	25 kcal (105 kj)
Aubergine	(l)	18 kcal (75 kj)
Avocado	(l)	54 kcal (227 kj)

B

Bacon (back rasher)	(l)*	53 kcal (222 kj)
Bagel	(h)	68 kcal (286 kj)
Baguette	(h)	77 kcal (323 kj)
Baked beans	(l)	23 kcal (97 kj)
Baked potato	(h)	21 kcal (88 kj)
Banana	(m)	26 kcal (110 kj)
Barley bread (no grains)	(m)	48 kcal (202 kj)
Barley bread (with grains)	(l)	44 kcal (184 kj)
Basmati rice (dried)	(m)	97 kcal (407 kj)
Basmati rice (cooked)	(m)	36 kcal (151 kj)

Beans and pulses

Baked beans	(l)	23 kcal (97 kj)
Black-eyed beans (dried)	(l)	77 kcal (323 kj)
Black-eyed beans (canned)	(l)	32 kcal (134 kj)
Broad beans (fresh)	(h)	17 kcal (71 kj)
Broad beans (canned)	(h)	25 kcal (105 kj)
Butter beans (dried)	(l)	83 kcal (349 kj)
Butter beans (canned)	(l)	22 kcal (92 kj)
Chana dhal	(l)	30 kcal (125 kj)
Chickpeas (dried)	(l)	91 kcal (382 kj)
Chickpeas (canned)	(l)	33 kcal (139 kj)
Flageolet beans	(l)	25 kcal (105 kj)
Haricot beans (dried)	(l)	82 kcal (344 kj)
Haricot beans (cooked)	(l)	27 kcal (113 kj)
Kidney beans (dried)	(l)	76 kcal (320 kj)
Kidney beans (canned)	(l)	29 kcal (121 kj)
Lentils (dried)	(l)	90 kcal (378 kj)
Lentils (canned)	(l)	30 kcal (126 kj)
Split peas (dried)	(l)	94 kcal (395 kj)
Split peas (cooked)	(l)	36 kcal (151 kj)
Soya beans (dried)	(l)	106 kcal (445 kj)
Soya beans (cooked)	(l)	40 kcal (168 kj)

Bean sprouts	(l)	9 kcal (38 kj)
Beef (lean cuts)	(l)*	50 kcal (210 kj)
Beef mince (lean)	(l)*	50 kcal (210 kj)
Beer	(h)	32 kcal (134 kj)
Beetroot	(m)	10 kcal (42 kj)

Biscuits and crackers

Cream crackers	(m)	124 kcal (520 kj)
Digestive biscuits	(m)	150 kcal (630 kj)
Melba toast	(h)	99 kcal (416 kj)
Oatcakes	(m)	123 kcal (516 kj)
Rice cakes	(h)	92 kcal (386 kj)
Rye crispbreads	(m)	88 kcal (370 kj)
Shortbread	(m)	120 kcal (504 kj)
Tea biscuits	(m)	112 kcal (470 kj)

Black-eyed beans (dried)	(l)	77 kcal (323 kj)
Black-eyed beans (canned)	(l)	32 kcal (134 kj)
Blackberries	(l)	7 kcal (29 kj)
Blueberries	(l)	8 kcal (34 kj)
Boiled potatoes	(l)	21 kcal (88 kj)
Boiled sweets	(h)	100 kcal (420 kj)
Bran cereal (flakes)	(h)	90 kcal (378 kj)

Bran cereal (noodle shaped)	(l)	76 kcal (320 kj)
Bran cereal (with fruit)	(m)	90 kcal (378 kj)
Brazil nuts	(l)	198 kcal (831 kj)

Bread and cakes

Bagel	(h)	68 kcal (286 kj)
Baguette	(h)	77 kcal (323 kj)
Barley bread (no grains)	(m)	48 kcal (202 kj)
Barley bread (with grain)	(l)	44 kcal (184 kj)
Bread stuffing (made-up)	(h)	35 kcal (147 kj)
Brown bread	(m)	62 kcal (260 kj)
Croissant	(m)	80 kcal (336 kj)
Crumpet	(m)	45 kcal (189 kj)
Doughnut	(h)	99 kcal (416 kj)
Fruit bread	(l)	85 kcal (357 kj)
Gluten-free bread	(h)	100 kcal (420 kj)
Granary bread	(l)	61 kcal (256 kj)
Muffin (plain)	(m)	90 kcal (378 kj)
Muffin (fruit)	(m)	100 kcal (420 kj)
Pancakes	(m)	73 kcal (307 kj)
Pastry	(m)	130 kcal (546 kj)
Pitta bread (white)	(m)	62 kcal (260 kj)
Pitta bread (brown)	(m)	61 kcal (256 kj)
Rye/pumpernickel bread (with grains)	(l)	46 kcal (193 kj)
Rye/pumpernickel (no grains)	(m)	90 kcal (378 kj)
Scones (plain)	(h)	75 kcal (315 kj)
Stoneground bread	(m)	60 kcal (252 kj)
Sourdough bread	(m)	63 kcal (264 kj)
Soya bread	(l)	64 kcal (269 kj)
Sponge cake	(l)	81 kcal (340 kj)
Tortilla wraps (white)	(m)	81 kcal (340 kj)
Tortilla wraps (wheat)	(l)	79 kcal (331 kj)
Waffles	(h)	110 kcal (462 kj)
White bread	(h)	62 kcal (260 kj)
White bread (added fibre)	(m)	61 kcal (256 kj)
Wholemeal bread	(m)	61 kcal (256 kj)

Breakfast cereals

Bran cereal (flakes)	(l)	90 kcal (378 kj)
Bran cereal (with fruit)	(m)	90 kcal (378 kj)
Bran cereal (noodle shaped)	(l)	76 kcal (320 kj)
Cornflakes	(h)	105 kcal (441 kj)
Honey-coated cereals	(h)	106 kcal (445 kj)
Muesli	(m)	105 kcal (441 kj)
Muesli (low sugar)	(m)	101 kcal (424 kj)
Porridge oats (dried)	(l)	105 kcal (441 kj)
Porridge (instant, dried)	(m)	111 kcal (466 kj)
Rice cereal	(h)	93 kcal (390 kj)
Wheat cereal	(h)	95 kcal (399 kj)

Broad beans (fresh)	(h)	17 kcal (71 kj) 74 g
Broad beans (canned)	(h)	25 kcal (105 kj)
Broccoli	(l)	9 kcal (38 kj) g
Brown bread	(m)	62 kcal (260 kj)
Brown rice (dried)	(m)	100 kcal (420 kj)
Brown rice (cooked)	(m)	40 kcal (168 kj)
Brussels sprouts	(l)	12 kcal (50 kj)
Buckwheat (dried)	(l)	102 kcal (428 kj)
Bulgar wheat (dried)	(l)	104 kcal (437 kj)
Butter	(l)	206 kcal (865 kj)
Butter beans (dried)	(l)	83 kcal (349 kj)
Butter beans (canned)	(l)	22 kcal (92 kj)

C

Cabbage	(l)	8 kcal (37 kj)
Camembert	(l)*	85 kcal (357 kj)
Cantaloupe	(m)	5 kcal (21 kj)
Capers	(l)	8 kcal (37 kj)
Carrots	(l)	10 kcal (42 kj)
Carrot juice	(l)	27 kcal (113 kj)
Cashew nuts	(l)	176 kcal (740 kj)
Cauliflower	(l)	10 kcal (42 kj)
Celery	(l)	2 kcal (8 kj)
Chana dhal	(l)	30 kcal (125 kj)
Cheddar	(l)*	116 kcal (487 kj)
Cheddar (half fat)	(l)*	75 kcal (315 kj)

Cheeses

Camembert	(l)*	85 kcal (357 kj)
Cheddar	(l)*	116 kcal (487 kj)
Cheddar (half fat)	(l)*	75 kcal (315 kj)
Cottage cheese	(l)*	27 kcal (113 kj)
Cottage cheese (half fat)	(l)*	22 kcal (92 kj)
Cream cheese	(l)*	80 kcal (336 kj)
Cream cheese (half fat)	(l)*	50 kcal (210 kj)
Edam	(l)*	95 kcal (399 kj)
Edam (half fat)	(l)*	70 kcal (294 kj)
Feta	(l)*	75 kcal (315 kj)
Mozzarella	(l)*	88 kcal (369 kj)
Parmesan	(l)*	108 kcal (453 kj)
Ricotta	(l)*	53 kcal (222 kj)
Stilton	(l)*	101 kcal (424 kj)

Cherries	(l)	11 kcal (46 kj)
Chicken (meat only)	(l)*	32 kcal (134 kj)
Chicken (meat and skin)	(l)*	37 kcal (155 kj)
Chicken nuggets	(l)	43 kcal (180 kj)
Chickpeas (dried)	(l)	91 kcal (382 kj)
Chickpeas (canned)	(l)	33 kcal (139 kj)
Chocolate (milk)	(l)	153 kcal (643 kj)
Chocolate (plain)	(l)	128 kcal (535 kj)
Chocolate (white)	(l)	150 kcal (630 kj)
Chocolate milk drink (low-fat)	(l)	81 kcal (340 kj)
Chocolate-covered peanuts	(l)	128 kcal (537 kj)
Chocolate spread	(l)	154 kcal (647 kj)
Cod fillet	(l)*	21 kcal (88 kj)
Cola	(m)	43 kcal (181 kj)
Condensed milk	(m)	17 kcal (71 kj)
Corn chips	(m)	57 kcal (249 kj)
Cornflakes	(h)	105 kcal (441 kj)
Corn-on-the-cob	(m)	19 kcal (80 kj)
Cottage cheese	(l)*	27 kcal (113 kj)
Cottage cheese (half fat)	(l)*	22 kcal (92 kj)
Courgette	(l)	5 kcal (21 kj)
Couscous (dried)	(m)	103 kcal (433 kj)
Couscous (cooked)	(m)	48 kcal (201 kj)
Crab meat	(l)*	37 kcal (155 kj)
Cranberry juice	(m)	51 kcal (214 kj)
Cream cheese	(l)*	80 kcal (336 kj)
Cream cheese (half fat)	(l)*	50 kcal (210 kj)
Cream crackers	(m)	80 kcal (336 kj)
Crème fraîche	(l)	48 kcal (201 kj)
Crisps (potato)	(m)	140 kcal (588 kj)
Croissant	(m)	80 kcal (336 kj)
Crumpet	(m)	45 kcal (189 kj)
Cucumber	(l)	3 kcal (13 kj)
Custard (25 g/1 oz powder made with skimmed milk)	(l)	22 kcal (92 kj)
Custard (25 g/1 oz powder made with whole milk)	(l)	33 kcal (139 kj)

D

Dairy products

Chocolate milk (low-fat)	(l)	81 kcal (340 kj)
Crème fraîche	(l)	48 kcal (201 kj)
Condensed milk	(m)	17 kcal (71 kj)
Ice cream (low-fat)	(l)	42 kcal (176 kj)
Ice cream (full fat)	(m)	70 kcal (294 kj)
Semi-skimmed milk	(l)	45 kcal (189 kj)
Skimmed milk	(l)	34 kcal (142 kj)

Soured cream	ⓛ	188 kcal (789 kj)
Whole milk	ⓛ	65 kcal (273 kj)
Yogurt	ⓛ	23 kcal (97 kj)
Yogurt (low-fat)	ⓛ	15 kcal (63 kj)
Dates (fresh)	ⓗ	31 kcal (130 kj)
Dates (dried)	ⓗ	77 kcal (323 kj)
Digestive biscuits	ⓜ	150 kcal (630 kj)
Doughnuts	ⓗ	99 kcal (416 kj)
Drinks		
Apple juice	ⓛ	43 kcal (180 kj)
Beer	ⓗ	32 kcal (134 kj)
Carrot juice	ⓛ	27 kcal (113 kj)
Chocolate milk (low-fat)	ⓛ	81 kcal (340 kj)
Cola	ⓜ	43 kcal (181 kj)
Cranberry juice	ⓜ	51 kcal (214 kj)
Glucose drinks	ⓗ	76 kcal (320 kj)
Grapefruit juice	ⓛ	35 kcal (147 kj)
Lemon squash (1 tablespoon, made-up)	ⓜ	20 kcal (84 kj)
Orange juice	ⓛ	40 kcal (168 kj)
Orange squash (1 tablespoon, made-up)	ⓜ	20 kcal (84 kj)
Orange drink (fizzy)	ⓛ	43 kcal (181 kj)
Pineapple juice	ⓛ	45 kcal (189 kj)
Sports drinks	ⓛ	28 kcal (118 kj)
Tomato juice	ⓛ	15 kcal (63 kj)
Water	ⓛ	0 kcal (0 kj)
Wine (white)	ⓜ	66 kcal (277 kj)
Wine (red)	ⓜ	68 kcal (285 kj)
Duck (meat only)	ⓛ*	53 kcal (223 kj)
Duck (meat and skin)	ⓛ*	94 kcal (395 kj)

E

Edam	ⓛ*	95 kcal (399 kj)
Edam (half fat)	ⓛ*	70 kcal (294 kj)
Eggs (medium)	ⓛ*	80 kcal (336 kj)
Egg noodles	ⓛ	109 kcal (458 kj)
Egg white	ⓛ*	15 kcal (63 kj)

F

Falafel	ⓛ	37 kcal (155 kj)
Feta	ⓛ*	75 kcal (315 kj)
Fettucine (white, dried)	ⓛ	103 kcal (432 kj)
Fettucine (white, cooked)	ⓛ	33 kcal (138 kj)
Figs (fresh)	ⓜ	12 kcal (50 kj)
Figs (dried)	ⓜ	65 kcal (273 kj)
Fish and shellfish		
Anchovies	ⓛ*	76 kcal (320 kj)
Cod fillet	ⓛ*	21 kcal (88 kj)
Crab meat	ⓛ*	37 kcal (155 kj)
Fish fingers	ⓛ	44 kcal (185 kj)
Haddock	ⓛ*	20 kcal (84 kj)
Halibut	ⓛ*	29 kcal (122 kj)

Kipper	ⓛ*	46 kcal (193 kj)
Lobster	ⓛ*	33 kcal (139 kj)
Mackerel	ⓛ*	62 kcal (260 kj)
Monkfish	ⓛ*	18 kcal (76 kj)
Mussels (shelled)	ⓛ*	25 kcal (105 kj)
Mussels (with shells)	ⓛ*	9 kcal (38 kj)
Pilchards	ⓛ*	40 kcal (168 kj)
Plaice	ⓛ*	27 kcal (113 kj)
Prawns (peeled)	ⓛ*	30 kcal (126 kj)
Salmon (fresh)	ⓛ*	50 kcal (210 kj)
Salmon (canned)	ⓛ*	44 kcal (185 kj)
Sardines (fresh)	ⓛ*	46 kcal (193 kj)
Sardines (canned in oil)	ⓛ*	61 kcal (256 kj)
Scallops	ⓛ*	21 kcal (88 kj)
Sole fillet	ⓛ*	26 kcal (109 kj)
Swordfish	ⓛ*	31 kcal (130 kj)
Trout fillet	ⓛ*	38 kcal (160 kj)
Tuna (fresh)	ⓛ*	40 kcal (168 kj)
Tuna (canned in spring water)	ⓛ*	28 kcal (118 kj)
Tuna (canned in oil)	ⓛ*	53 kcal (223 kj)
Fish fingers	ⓛ	44 kcal (185 kj)
French fries (thick cut)	ⓗ	54 kcal (227 kj)
French fries (thin cut)	ⓗ	80 kcal (336 kj)
Fruits		
Apple	ⓛ	13 kcal (55 kj)
Apricots	ⓜ	8 kcal (34 kj)
Apricots (canned)	ⓜ	18 kcal (76 kj)
Apricots (dried)	ⓛ	53 kcal (223 kj)
Avocado	ⓛ	54 kcal (227 kj)
Banana		26 kcal (110 kj)
Blackberries	ⓛ	7 kcal (29 kj)
Blueberries	ⓛ	8 kcal (34 kj)
Cantaloupe	ⓜ	5 kcal (21 kj)
Cherries	ⓛ	11 kcal (46 kj)
Figs (fresh)	ⓜ	12 kcal (50 kj)
Figs (dried)	ⓜ	65 kcal (273 kj)
Fruit cocktail (canned in juice)	ⓜ	8 kcal (34 kj)
Fruit cocktail (canned in syrup)	ⓜ	16 kcal (68 kj)
Grapefruit	ⓛ	9 kcal (38 kj)
Grapes (white)	ⓛ	16 kcal (67 kj)
Grapes (red)	ⓜ	16 kcal (67 kj)
Kiwi fruit	ⓛ	12 kcal (50 kj)
Lemons	ⓛ	4 kcal (17 kj)
Limes	ⓛ	2 kcal (8 kj)
Mandarin	ⓛ	11 kcal (46 kj)
Mango	ⓜ	16 kcal (67 kj)
Olives	ⓛ	34 kcal (143 kj)

Oranges	ⓛ	7 kcal (30 kj)
Papaya	ⓜ	10 kcal (42 kj)
Peaches	ⓛ	8 kcal (34 kj)
Peaches (canned in juice)	ⓛ	11 kcal (46 kj)
Peaches (canned in syrup)	ⓜ	16 kcal (67 kj)
Pears	ⓛ	12 kcal (50 kj)
Pears (canned in juice)	ⓛ	9 kcal (38 kj)
Pears (canned in syrup)	ⓜ	14 kcal (59 kj)
Pineapple	ⓜ	12 kcal (50 kj)
Pineapple (canned in juice)	ⓜ	13 kcal (55 kj)
Pineapple (canned in syrup)	ⓜ	18 kcal (76 kj)
Plums	ⓛ	10 kcal (420 kj)
Prunes	ⓛ	38 kcal (160 kj)
Raisins	ⓜ	78 kcal (328 kj)
Raspberries	ⓛ	7 kcal (29 kj)
Satsumas	ⓛ	11 kcal (46 kj)
Strawberries	ⓛ	8 kcal (34 kj)
Sultanas	ⓜ	79 kcal (332 kj)
Watermelon (with skin)	ⓗ	5 kcal (21 kj)
Watermelon (skinned)	ⓗ	9 kcal (38 kj)
Tomatoes	ⓛ	5 kcal (21 kj)
Tomatoes (canned)	ⓛ	5 kcal (21 kj)
Fruit bread	ⓜ	85 kcal (357 kj)
Fruit cocktail (canned in juice)	ⓜ	8 kcal (34 kj)
Fruit cocktail (canned in syrup)	ⓜ	16 kcal (68 kj)

G

Gammon steak (fat removed)	ⓛ*	47 kcal (197 kj)
Gluten-free bread	ⓗ	100 kcal (420 kj)
Gluten-free pasta	ⓜ	100 kcal (420 kj)
Glucose drinks	ⓗ	76 kcal (320 kj)
Goose	ⓛ*	89 kcal (374 kj)
Granary bread	ⓛ	61 kcal (256 kj)
Grapefruit	ⓛ	9 kcal (38 kj)
Grapefruit juice	ⓛ	35 kcal (147 kj)
Grapes (white)	ⓛ	16 kcal (67 kj)
Grapes (red)	ⓜ	16 kcal (67 kj)
Guacamole	ⓛ	53 kcal (222 kj)

H

Haddock	ⓛ*	20 kcal (84 kj)
Halibut	ⓛ*	29 kcal (122 kj)
Ham (reduced fat)	ⓛ*	32 kcal (134 kj)
Hamburger roll	ⓜ	80 kcal (336 kj)
Haricot beans (dried)	ⓛ	82 kcal (344 kj)
Haricot beans (cooked)	ⓛ	27 kcal (113 kj)

Honey (m) 85 kcal (357 kJ)

Honey-coated cereal (h) 106 kcal (445 kJ)

Hummus (l) 85 kcal (357 kJ)

I

Ice cream (low-fat) (l) 42 kcal (176 kJ)

Ice cream (full fat) (m) 70 kcal (294 kJ)

Instant noodles (l) 85 kcal (357 kJ)

Instant mash (dried) (h) 90 kcal (378 kJ)

Instant mash (reconstituted) (h) 15 kcal (63 kJ)

J

Jam (l) 75 kcal (315 kJ)

Jasmine rice (h) 98 kcal (412 kJ)

Jelly beans (h) 92 kcal (386 kJ)

K

Kidney beans (dried) (l) 76 kcal (320 kJ)

Kidney beans (canned) (l) 29 kcal (121 kJ)

Kippers (l)* 46 kcal (193 kJ)

Kiwi fruit (l) 12 kcal (50 kJ)

L

Lamb chop (with fat) (l)* 88 kcal (370 kJ)

Lamb (lean) (l)* 57 kcal (240 kJ)

Leeks (l) 6 kcal (25 kJ)

Lemon squash (m) 20 kcal (84 kJ)
(1 tablespoon, made-up)

Lemons (l) 4 kcal (17 kJ)

Lentils (dried) (l) 90 kcal (378 kJ)

Lentils (canned) (l) 30 kcal (126 kJ)

Lentil soup (l) 23 kcal (97 kJ)

Lettuce (l) 4 kcal (17 kJ)

Limes (l) 2 kcal (8 kJ)

Linguine (dried) (l) 103 kcal (432 kJ)

Lobster (l)* 33 kcal (139 kJ)

Low-fat spread (l) 106 kcal (445 kJ)

M

Mackerel (l)* 62 kcal (260 kJ)

Mandarin (l) 11 kcal (46 kJ)

Margarine (l) 204 kcal (856 kJ)

Mashed potato (real) (h) 21 kcal (88 kJ)

Mashed potato (instant) (h) 15 kcal (63 kJ)

Macaroni (l) 103 kcal (432 kJ)

Mangetout (l) 9 kcal (37 kJ)

Mango (m) 16 kcal (67 kJ)

Marmalade (l) 72 kcal (30 kJ)

Meats

  Bacon (back rasher) (l)* 53 kcal (222 kJ)

Beef (lean cuts) (l)* 50 kcal (210 kJ)

Beef mince (lean) (l)* 50 kcal (210 kJ)

Gammon steak (fat removed) (l)* 47 kcal (197 kJ)

Ham (reduced fat) (l)* 32 kcal (134 kJ)

Lamb chop (with fat) (l)* 88 kcal (370 kJ)

Lamb (lean) (l)* 57 kcal (240 kJ)

Pork (meat only) (l)* 59 kcal (248 kJ)

Pork chop (lean) (l)* 53 kcal (223 kJ)

Pork chop (with fat) (l)* 73 kcal (307 kJ)

Sausages (l) 80 kcal (336 kJ)

Sirloin steak (l)* 54 kcal (227 kJ)

Venison (l)* 30 kcal (126 kJ)

Veal (l)* 65 kcal (273 kJ)

Melba toast (h) 99 kcal (416 kJ)

Millet (h) 104 kcal (437 kJ)

Minestrone soup (l) 11 kcal (46 kJ)

Milks

  Condensed milk (m) 17 kcal (71 kJ)

  Chocolate milk (low-fat) (l) 81 kcal (340 kJ)

  Semi-skimmed (l) 45 kcal (189 kJ)

  Skimmed (l) 34 kcal (142 kJ)

  Soya milk (l) 43 kcal (180 kJ)

  Whole milk (l) 65 kcal (273 kJ)

Monkfish (l)* 18 kcal (76 kJ)

Mozzarella (l)* 88 kcal (369 kJ)

Muesli (m) 105 kcal (441 kJ)

Muesli (low sugar) (m) 101 kcal (424 kJ)

Muesli bars (m) 101 kcal (424 kJ)

Muffin (plain) (m) 90 kcal (378 kJ)

Muffin (fruit) (m) 100 kcal (420 kJ)

Mussels (shelled) (l)* 25 kcal (105 kJ)

Mussels (with shells) (l)* 9 kcal (38 kJ)

N

Nut oils (l) 899 kcal (3775 kJ)

O

Oatcakes (m) 123 kcal (516 kJ)

Oils and fats

  Butter (l) 206 kcal (865 kJ)

  Low-fat spread (l) 106 kcal (445 kJ)

  Margarine (l) 204 kcal (856 kJ)

  Nut oils (l) 899 kcal (3775 kJ)

  Olive oil (l) 899 kcal (3775 kJ)

  Vegetable oil (l) 900 kcal (3780 kJ)

Olives (l) 34 kcal (143 kJ)

Olive oil (l) 899 kcal (3775 kJ)

Onions (l) 10 kcal (420 kJ)

Oranges (l) 7 kcal (30 kJ)

Orange juice (l) 40 kcal (168 kJ)

Orange squash (m) 20 kcal (84 kJ)
(1 tablespoon, made-up)

Orange drink (fizzy) (m) 43 kcal (181 kJ)

P

Pancakes (m) 73 kcal (307 kJ)

Papaya (m) 10 kcal (420 kJ)

Parmesan (l)* 108 kcal (453 kJ)

Parsnips (h) 18 kcal (76 kJ)

Pasta, rice and grains

  Basmati rice (dried) (m) 97 kcal (407 kJ)

  Basmati rice (cooked) (m) 36 kcal (151 kJ)

  Brown rice (dried) (m) 100 kcal (420 kJ)

  Brown rice (cooked) (m) 40 kcal (168 kJ)

  Buckwheat (dried) (l) 102 kcal (428 kJ)

  Bulgar wheat (dried) (l) 104 kcal (437 kJ)

  Couscous (dried) (m) 103 kcal (433 kJ)

  Couscous (cooked) (m) 48 kcal (201 kJ)

  Egg noodles (l) 109 kcal (458 kJ)

  Fettucine (white, dried) (l) 103 kcal (432 kJ)

  Fettucine (white, cooked) (l) 33 kcal (138 kJ)

  Gluten-free pasta (m) 100 kcal (420 kJ)

  Instant noodles (l) 85 kcal (357 kJ)

  Jasmine rice (h) 98 kcal (412 kJ)

  Linguine (dried) (l) 103 kcal (432 kJ)

  Macaroni (l) 103 kcal (432 kJ)

  Millet (h) 104 kcal (437 kJ)

  Pearl Barley (l) 101 kcal (424 kJ)

  Quinoa (l) 87 kcal (365 kJ)

  Ravioli (meat, dried) (l) 78 kcal (328 kJ)

  Ravioli (meat, cooked) (l) 46 kcal (193 kJ)

  Ravioli (cheese, dried) (l) 95 kcal (399 kJ)

  Ravioli (cheese, cooked) (l) 57 kcal (238 kJ)

  Risotto rice (m) 101 kcal (424 kJ)

  Spaghetti (white, dried) (l) 103 kcal (432 kJ)

  Spaghetti (white, cooked) (l) 33 kcal (138 kJ)

  Spaghetti (brown, dried) (l) 96 kcal (403 kJ)

  Spaghetti (brown, cooked) (l) 32 kcal (134 kJ)

  Tortellini (meat, dried) (l) 78 kcal (328 kJ)

Tortellini (meat, cooked) — (l) 46 kcal (193 kj)

Tortellini (cheese, dried) — (l) 95 kcal (399 kj)

Tortellini (cheese, cooked) — (l) 57 kcal (238 kj)

Udon noodles — (m) 86 kcal (361 kj)

Vermicelli (dried) — (l) 103 kcal (433 kj)

Vermicelli (cooked) — (l) 34 kcal (143 kj)

White rice (dried) — (m) 108 kcal (453 kj)

White rice (cooked) — (m) 39 kcal (164 kj)

White rice (fast cook, dried) — (h) 108 kcal (453 kj)

White rice (fast cook, cooked) — (h) 39 kcal (164 kj)

Wild rice (dried) — (m) 104 kcal (437 kj)

Wild rice (cooked) — (m) 50 kcal (210 kj)

Pastry — (m) 130 kcal (546 kj)

Pâté — (l) 85 kcal (357 kj)

Pâté (low-fat) — (l) 50 kcal (210 kj)

Peaches — (l) 8 kcal (34 kj)

Peaches (canned in syrup) — (m) 16 kcal (67 kj)

Peanuts — (l) 160 kcal (672 kj)

Peanuts (chocolate-covered) — (l) 128 kcal (537 kj)

Peanut butter — (l) 150 kcal (630 kj)

Pearl barley — (l) 101 kcal (424 kj)

Pears — (l) 12 kcal (50 kj)

Pears (canned in juice) — (l) 9 kcal (38 kj)

Peas — (l) 24 kcal (100 kj)

Peppers — (l) 5 kcal (21 kj)

Pilchards — (l)* 40 kcal (168 kj)

Pineapple — (m) 12 kcal (50 kj)

Pineapple (canned in juice) — (m) 13 kcal (55 kj)

Pineapple (canned in syrup) — (m) 18 kcal (76 kj)

Pineapple juice — (m) 45 kcal (189 kj)

Pinenuts — (l) 193 kcal (810 kj)

Pitta bread (white) — (m) 80 kcal (336 kj)

Pitta bread (brown) — (m) 80 kcal (336 kj)

Pizza (meat, thin crust) — (l) 62 kcal (260 kj)

Pizza (vegetarian, thin crust) — (l) 58 kcal (244 kj)

Plaice — (l)* 27 kcal (113 kj)

Plums — (l) 10 kcal (420 kj)

Popcorn — (l) 100 kcal (420kg

Pork (meat only) — (l)* 59 kcal (248 kj)

Pork chop (lean) — (l)* 53 kcal (223 kj)

Pork chop (with fat) — (l)* 73 kcal (307 kj)

Porridge oats (dried) — (l) 105 kcal (441 kj)

Porridge (instant, dried) — (m) 111 kcal (466 kj)

Potatoes

Baked — (h) 21 kcal (88 kj)

Crisps — (m) 140 kcal (588 kj)

French fries (thick cut) — (h) 54 kcal (227 kj)

French fries (thin cut) — (h) 80 kcal (336 kj)

Mashed (real) — (h) 21 kcal (88 kj)

Mashed (instant) — (h) 15 kcal (63 kj)

New — (l) 20 kcal (84 kj)

Sweet potatoes — (m) 25 kcal (105 kj)

Yam — (m) 33 kcal (139 kj)

Poultry and game

Chicken (meat only) — (l)* 32 kcal (134 kj)

Chicken (meat and skin) — (l)* 37 kcal (155 kj)

Chicken nuggets L 43 kcal (180 kj)

Duck (meat only) — (l)* 53 kcal (223 kj)

Duck (meat and skin) — (l)* 94 kcal (395 kj)

Goose — (l)* 89 kcal (374 kj)

Turkey (meat only) — (l)* 45 kcal (189 kj)

Turkey (meat and skin) — (l)* 52 kcal (218 kj)

Prawns (peeled) — (l)* 30 kcal (126 kj)

Pretzels — (h) 91 kcal (382 kj)

Pumpkin — (h) 4 kcal (17 kj)

Pumpkin seeds — (l) 159 kcal (667 kj)

Q

Quinoa — (l) 87 kcal (365 kj)

Quorn™ — (l) 24 kcal (100 kj)

R

Raisins — (m) 78 kcal (328 kj)

Raspberries — (l) 7 kcal (29 kj)

Ravioli (meat, dried) — (l) 78 kcal (328 kj)

Ravioli (meat, cooked) — (l) 46 kcal (193 kj)

Ravioli (cheese, dried) — (l) 95 kcal (399 kj)

Ravioli (cheese, cooked) — (l) 57 kcal (238 kj)

Rice

Basmati (dried) — (m) 97 kcal (407 kj)

Basmati (cooked) — (m) 36 kcal (151 kj)

Brown rice (dried) — (m) 100 kcal (420 kj)

Brown rice (cooked) — (m) 40 kcal (168 kj)

Jasmine rice — (h) 98 kcal (412 kj)

Risotto rice — (m) 101 kcal (424 kj)

White (dried) — (m) 108 kcal (453 kj)

White (cooked) — (m) 39 kcal (164 kj)

White (fast cook, dried) — (h) 108 kcal (453 kj)

White (fast cook, cooked) — (h) 39 kcal (164 kj)

Wild rice (dried) — (m) 104 kcal (437 kj)

Wild rice (cooked) — (m) 50 kcal (210 kj)

Rice cakes — (h) 92 kcal (386 kj)

Rice cereal (plain) — (h) 100 kcal (420 kj)

Rice cereal (chocolate) — (h) 108 kcal (453 kj)

Rice noodles (dried) — (m) 102 kcal (428 kj)

Rice noodles (cooked) — (m) 35 kcal (147 kj)

Ricotta — (l)* 53 kcal (222 kj)

Risotto rice — (m) 101 kcal (424 kj)

Rice cereals — (h) 93 kcal (390 kj)

Rye bread (with grains) — (m) 46 kcal (193 kj)

Rye bread (no grains) — (h) 90 kcal (378 kj)

Rye crispbreads — (m) 88 kcal (370 kj)

S

Salmon (fresh) — (l)* 50 kcal (210 kj)

Salmon (canned) — (l)* 44 kcal (185 kj)

Salsa — (l) 13 kcal (55 kj)

Sardines (fresh) — (l)* 46 kcal (193 kj)

Sardines (canned in oil) — (l)* 61 kcal (256 kj)

Satsumas — (l) 11 kcal (46 kj)

Sausages — (l) 80 kcal (336 kj)

Scallops — (l)* 21 kcal (88 kj)

Scones (plain) — (h) 75 kcal (315 kj)

Semi-skimmed milk — (l) 45 kcal (189 kj)

Shortbread — (m) 120 kcal (504 kj)

Sirloin steak — (l)* 54 kcal (227 kj)

Skimmed milk — (l) 34 kcal (142 kj)

Sole fillet — (l)* 26 kcal (109 kj)

Snacks (savoury)

Almonds — (l) 172 kcal (722 kj)

Brazil nuts — (l) 198 kcal (831 kj)

Cashew nuts — (l) 176 kcal (740 kj)

Corn chips — (m) 57 kcal (249 kj)

Crisps (potato) — (m) 140 kcal (588 kj)

Peanuts — (l) 160 kcal (672 kj)

Popcorn — (h) 100 kcal (420kg)

Pretzels — (h) 91 kcal (382 kj)

Rice cakes — (h) 92 kcal (386 kj)

Walnuts — (l) 192 kcal (806 kj)

Snacks (sweet)

Boiled sweets — (h) 100 kcal (420 kj)

Chewy fruit sweets — (h) 105 kcal (441 kj)

Chocolate (milk) — (l) 153 kcal (643 kj)

Chocolate (plain) (l) 128 kcal (535 kj)
Chocolate (white) (l) 150 kcal (630 kj)
Chocolate-covered peanuts (l) 128 kcal (537 kj)
Digestive biscuits (m) 150 kcal (630 kj)
Doughnuts (h) 99 kcal (416 kj)
Ice cream (low-fat) (l) 42 kcal (176 kj)
Ice cream (full fat) (m) 70 kcal (294 kj)
Jelly beans (h) 92 kcal (386 kj)
Muesli bars (m) 101 kcal (424 kj)
Muffin (plain) (m) 90 kcal (378 kj)
Muffin (fruit) (m) 100 kcal (420 kj)
Shortbread (m) 120 kcal (504 kj)
Sponge cake (l) 81 kcal (340 kj)
Tea biscuits (m) 112 kcal (470 kj)
Yogurt (l) 23 kcal (97 kj)
Yogurt (low-fat) (l) 15 kcal (63 kj)
Soured cream (l) 188 kcal (789 kj)
Sourdough bread (m) 63 kcal (264 kj)
Soya beans (dried) (l) 106 kcal (445 kj)
Soy beans (cooked) (l) 40 kcal (168 kj)
Soya bread (l) 64 kcal (269 kj)
Soya milk (l) 43 kcal (180 kj)
Soya mince (granules) (l) 74 kcal (310 kj)
Spinach (l) 7 kcal (29 kj)
Split peas (dried) (l) 94 kcal (395 kj)
Split peas (cooked) (l) 36 kcal (151 kj)
Spaghetti (white, dried) (l) 103 kcal (432 kj)
Spaghetti (white, cooked) (l) 33 kcal (138 kj)
Spaghetti (brown, dried) (l) 96 kcal (403 kj)
Spaghetti (brown, cooked) (l) 32 kcal (134 kj)
Spreads and dips
Chocolate spread (l) 154 kcal (647 kj)
Honey (m) 85 kcal (357 kj)
Hummus (l) 85 kcal (357 kj)
Jam (l) 75 kcal (315 kj)
Marmalade (l) 72 kcal (30 kj)
Peanut butter (l) 150 kcal (630 kj)
Salsa (l) 13 kcal (55 kj)
Guacamole (l) 53 kcal (222 kj)
Sponge cake (l) 81 kcal (340 kj)
Sports drinks (h) 28 kcal (118 kj)
Strawberries (l) 8 kcal (34 kj)
Stilton (l)* 101 kcal (424 kj)
Stuffing (bread, made-up) (h) 35 kcal (147 kj)
Sultanas (m) 79 kcal (332 kj)

Swede (h) 7 kcal (29 kj)
Sweetcorn (m) 35kcal (147 kj)
Sweet potatoes (m) 25 kcal (105 kj)
Swordfish (l)* 31 kcal (130 kj)

T

Taco shells (m) 120 kcal (504 kj)
Tea biscuits (m) 112 kcal (470 kj)
Tofu (l) 34 kcal (142 kj)
Tomatoes (l) 5 kcal (21 kj)
Tomatoes (canned) (l) 5 kcal (21 kj)
Tomato juice (l) 15 kcal (63 kj)
Tomato soup (l) 16 kcal (67 kj)
Tortellini (meat, dried) (l) 78 kcal (328 kj)
Tortellini (meat, cooked) (l) 46 kcal (193 kj)
Tortellini (cheese, dried) (l) 95 kcal (399 kj)
Tortellini (cheese, cooked) (l) 57 kcal (238 kj)
Tortilla wraps (white) (m) 81 kcal (340 kj)
Tortilla wraps (wheat) (l) 79 kcal (331 kj)
Trout fillet (l)* 38 kcal (160 kj)
Tuna (fresh) (l)* 40 kcal (168 kj)
Tuna (canned in spring water) (l)* 28 kcal (118 kj)
Tuna (canned in oil) (l)* 53 kcal (223 kj)
Turkey (meat only) (l)* 45 kcal (189 kj)
Turkey (meat and skin) (l)* 52 kcal (218 kj)
Tzatziki (l) 18 kcal (75 kj)

U

Udon noodles (m) 86 kcal (361 kj)

V

Veal (l)* 65 kcal (273 kj)
Vegetables
Alfalfa (l) 7 kcal (29 kj)
Artichoke (l) 13 kcal (55 kj)
Asparagus (l) 25 kcal (105 kj)
Aubergine (l) 18 kcal (75 kj)
Bean sprouts (l) 9 kcal (38 kj)
Beetroot (m) 10 kcal (42 kj)
Broccoli (l) 9 kcal (38 kj)
Brussels sprouts (l) 12 kcal (50 kj)
Cabbage (l) 8 kcal (37 kj)
Capers (l) 8 kcal (37 kj)
Carrots (l) 10 kcal (42 kj)
Cauliflower (l) 10 kcal (42 kj)
Celery (l) 2 kcal (8 kj)
Corn-on-the-cob (m) 19 kcal (80 kj)
Courgette (l) 5 kcal (21 kj)
Cucumber (l) 3 kcal (13 kj)

Leeks (l) 6 kcal (25 kj)
Lettuce (l) 4 kcal (17 kj)
Mangetout (l) 9 kcal (37 kj)
Onions (l) 10 kcal (420 kj)
Parsnips (h) 18 kcal (76 kj)
Peas (l) 24 kcal (100 kj)
Peppers (l) 5 kcal (21 kj)
Pumpkin (h) 4 kcal (17 kj)
Spinach (l) 7 kcal (29 kj)
Swede (h) 7 kcal (29 kj)
Sweetcorn (m) 35 kcal (147 kj)
Tomatoes (l) 5 kcal (21 kj)
Tomatoes (canned) (l) 5 kcal (21 kj)
Watercress (l) 6 kcal (25 kj)
Vegetable oil (l) 900 kcal (3780 kj)
Venison (l)* 30 kcal (126 kj)
Vermicelli (dried) (l) 103 kcal (433 kj)
Vermicelli (cooked) (l) 34 kcal (143 kj)

W

Watercress (l) 6 kcal (25 kj)
Watermelon (with skin) (h) 5 kcal (21 kj)
Watermelon (skinless) (h) 9 kcal (38 kj)
Waffles (h) 110 kcal (462 kj)
Walnuts (l) 192 kcal (806 kj)
Wheat cereal (m) 95 kcal (399 kj)
Whey protein (l)* 4 kcal (17 kj)
White bread (h) 62 kcal (260 kj)
White bread (added fibre) (m) 61 kcal (256 kj)
White rice (dried) (m) 108 kcal (453 kj)
White rice (cooked) (m) 39 kcal (164 kj)
White rice (fast cook, dried) (h) 108 kcal (453 kj)
White rice (fast cook, cooked) (h) 39 kcal (164 kj)
Whole milk (l) 65 kcal (273 kj)
Wholegrain bread (m) 61 kcal (256 kj)
Wild rice (dried) (m) 104 kcal (437 kj)
Wild rice (cooked) (m) 50 kcal (210 kj)
Wine (white) (m) 66 kcal (277 kj)
Wine (red) (m) 68 kcal (285 kj)

Y

Yam (m) 33 kcal (139 kj)
Yogurt (l) 23 kcal (97 kj)
Yogurt (low-fat) (l) 15 kcal (63 kj)

index

acknowledgements

Thanks to all the commissioning editors who bore with me while I wrote
this book – particularly Simone Cave at the *Mirror* and Andrew Fleming at
Best. Also, Auckland nutritionist Dale Faddon, who answered many daft
questions, and nutritionists Natalie Savona, Lyndel Costain and Antony
Haynes who have answered many questions in the past. And thanks to
my mum, Martin and Tim as ever.

Bibliography

Jennie Brand Miller Phd, Thomas MS Wolever, MD Phd, Stephen Colagiuri,
MD and Kaye Foster-Powell, M.Nutr & Diet., *The Glucose Revolution*
(Marlowe & Company New York, 1966); Richard N Podell MD, FACP and
William Proctor, *The G-Index Diet* (Warner Books, New York, 1993); Dr Robert
Atkins, *Dr Atkins Age Defying Diet Revolution* (Bantam Books, New York,
2000, published by arrangement with St Martins Press); Leslie Kenton, *The
X Factor Diet* (Vermilion, London 2002)

Executive Editor	Nicky Hill
Editor	Rachel Lawrence
Executive Art Editor	Jo MacGregor
Designer	Ginny Zeal
Production	Louise Hall
Special Photography	Ian O'Leary and Lis Parsons
Food Stylists	Beth Heald and David Morgan